W. A. MOZART

Piano Concerto No. 27 in B-Flat Major, K. 595

To access audio visit:
www.halleonard.com/mylibrary

Enter Code
3722-8996-1221-7787

ISBN 978-1-59615-076-8

© 2001 MMO Music Group, Inc.
All Rights Reserved

For all works contained herein:
Unauthorized copying, arranging, adapting, recording, Internet posting, public performance,
or other distribution of the music in this publication is an infringement of copyright.
Infringers are liable under the law.

Visit Hal Leonard Online at
www.halleonard.com

Contact us:
Hal Leonard
7777 West Bluemound Road
Milwaukee, WI 53213
Email: info@halleonard.com

In Europe, contact:
Hal Leonard Europe Limited
42 Wigmore Street
Marylebone, London, W1U 2RN
Email: info@halleonardeurope.com

In Australia, contact:
Hal Leonard Australia Pty. Ltd.
4 Lentara Court
Cheltenham, Victoria, 3192 Australia
Email: info@halleonard.com.au

Wolfgang Amadeus
MOZART
CONCERTO No. 27
in B-flat major
for
Piano and Orchestra
KV595

CONCERTO Nº 27
FOR
PIANO AND ORCHESTRA
in B-flat major, KV 595

I

Wolfgang Amadeus Mozart
(1756-1791)

15
II
p

18
II

21
II

24
II
A
p

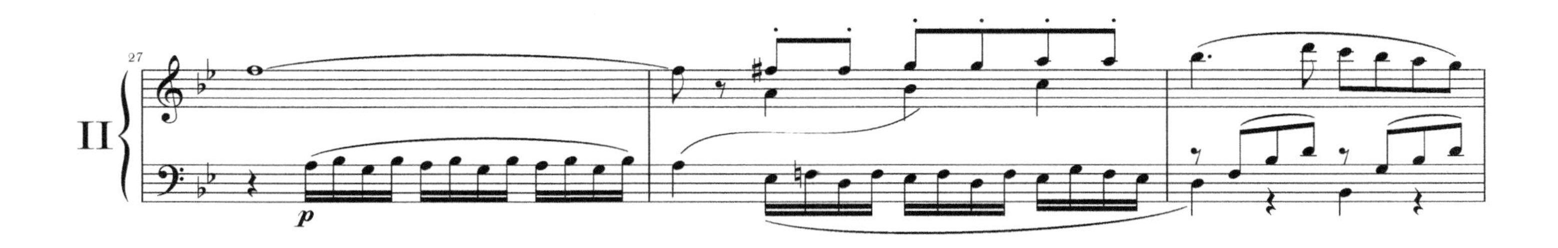
27
II
p

30
II
mf
p

34
II
mf
p

37
II
mf
p
pp

40
II
cresc.
f

43
II
pp
cresc.
sim.
f

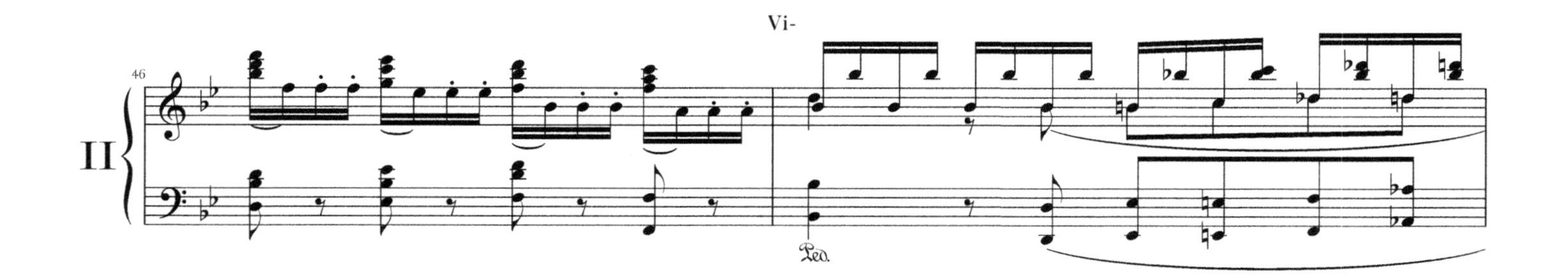
46
II
Vi-
Ped.

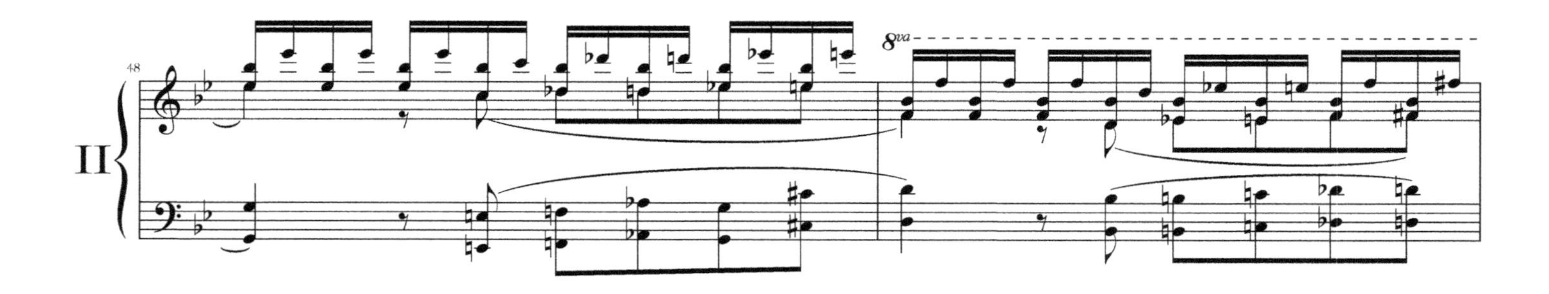
48
II
8va

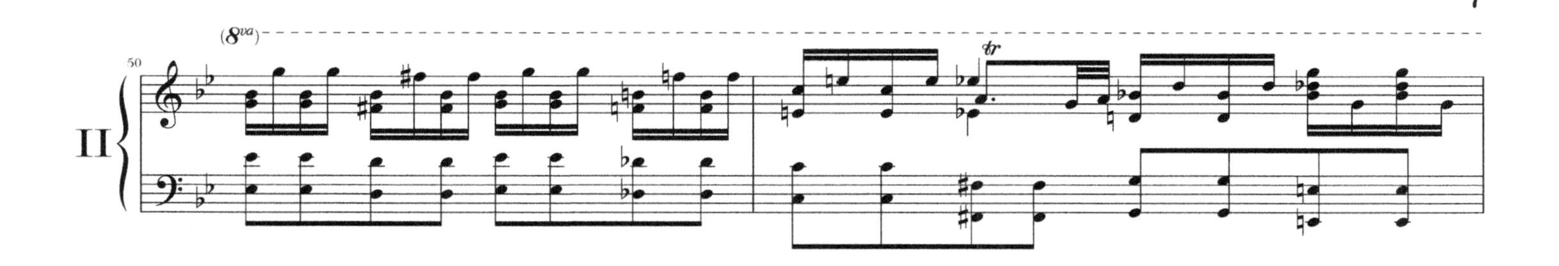
(8va)
50
II
tr

(8va)
52
II
-de
B
sf

55
II
p
sf
p

60
II

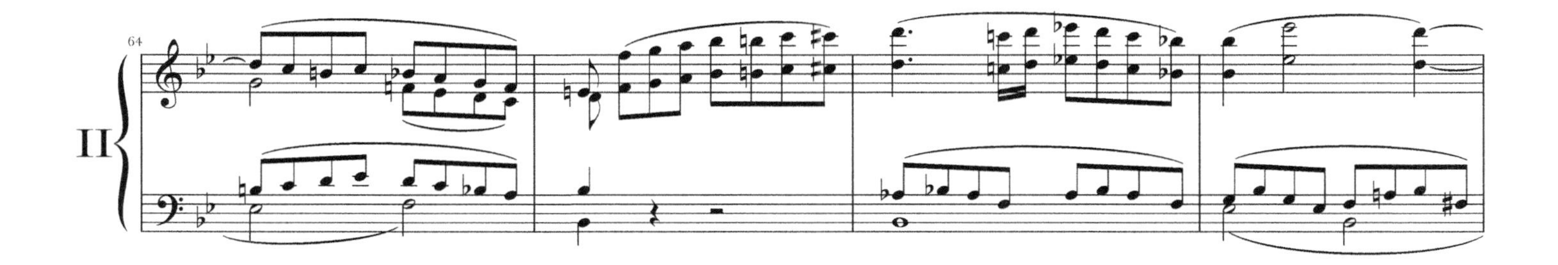
64
II

68
II

C
II

II

II

D
I
legato

I
Solo
II

88
I
II

92
I
II
Tutti
f

95
E
I
f
p
legato
II
Solo
p

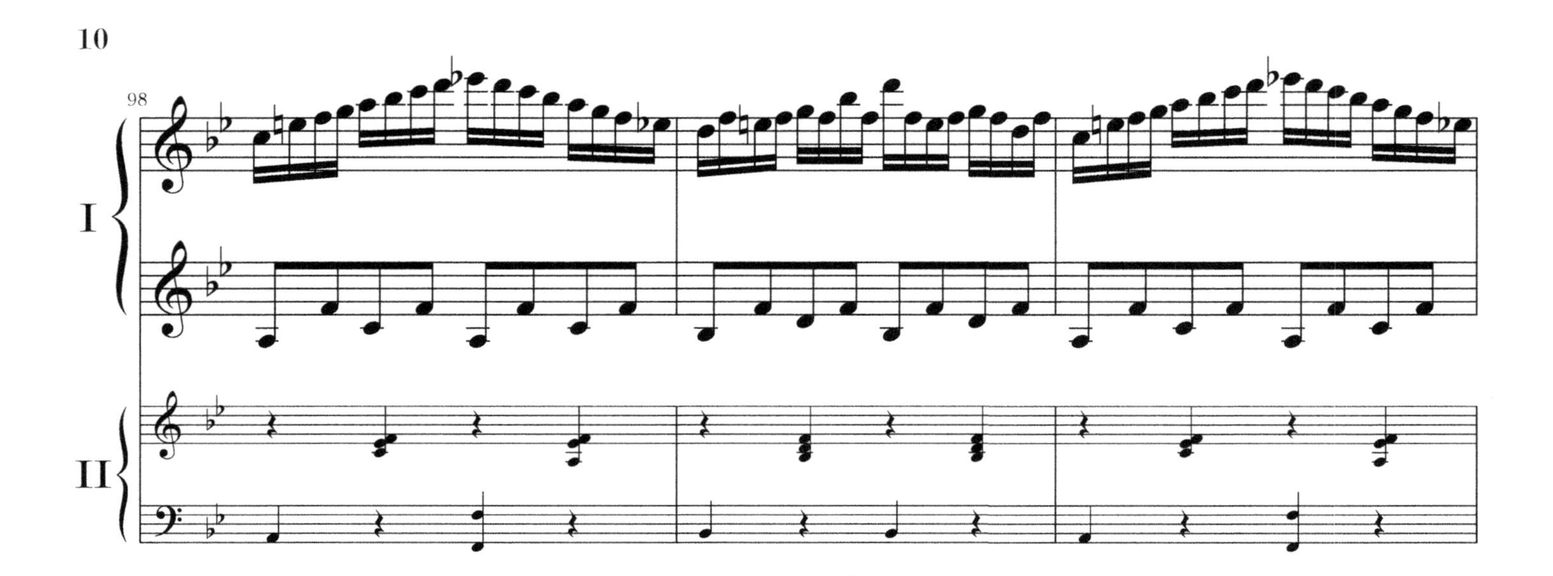
98
I
II

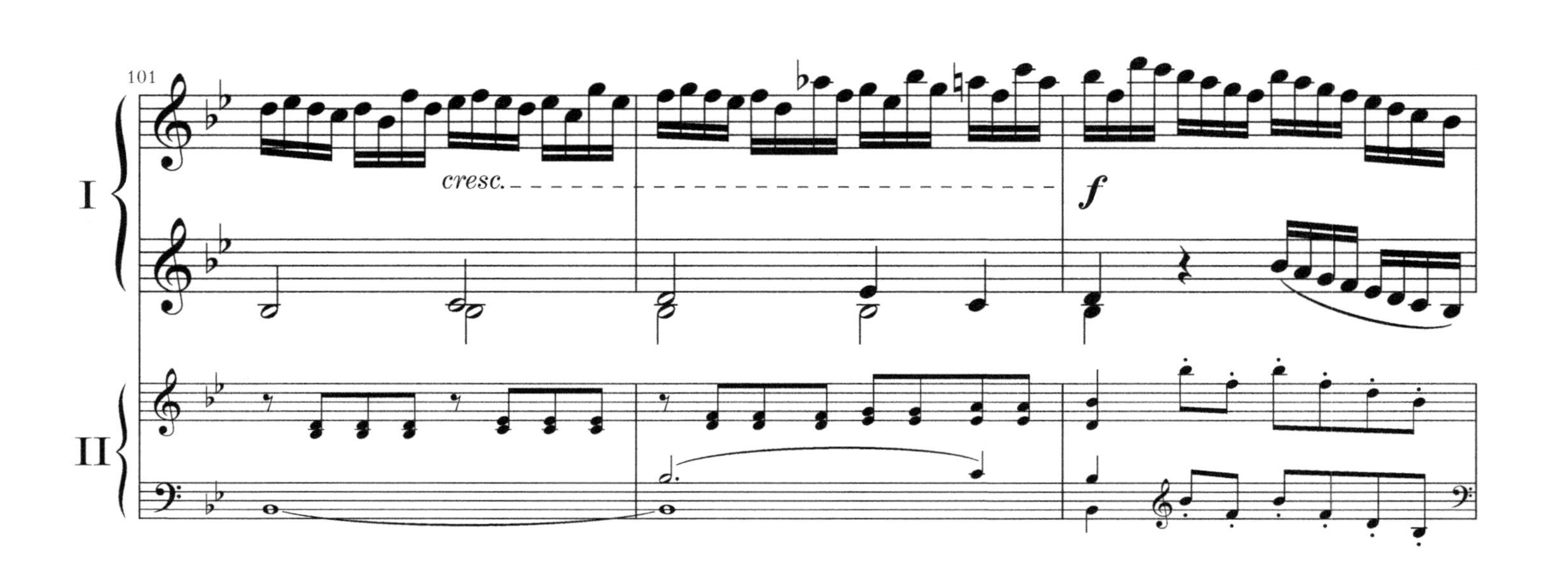
101
cresc.
f
I
II

104
F
p
sost.
tr
tr
I
Tutti
f
II

107
I
II
mf
Solo
p

111
I
II
p
tr

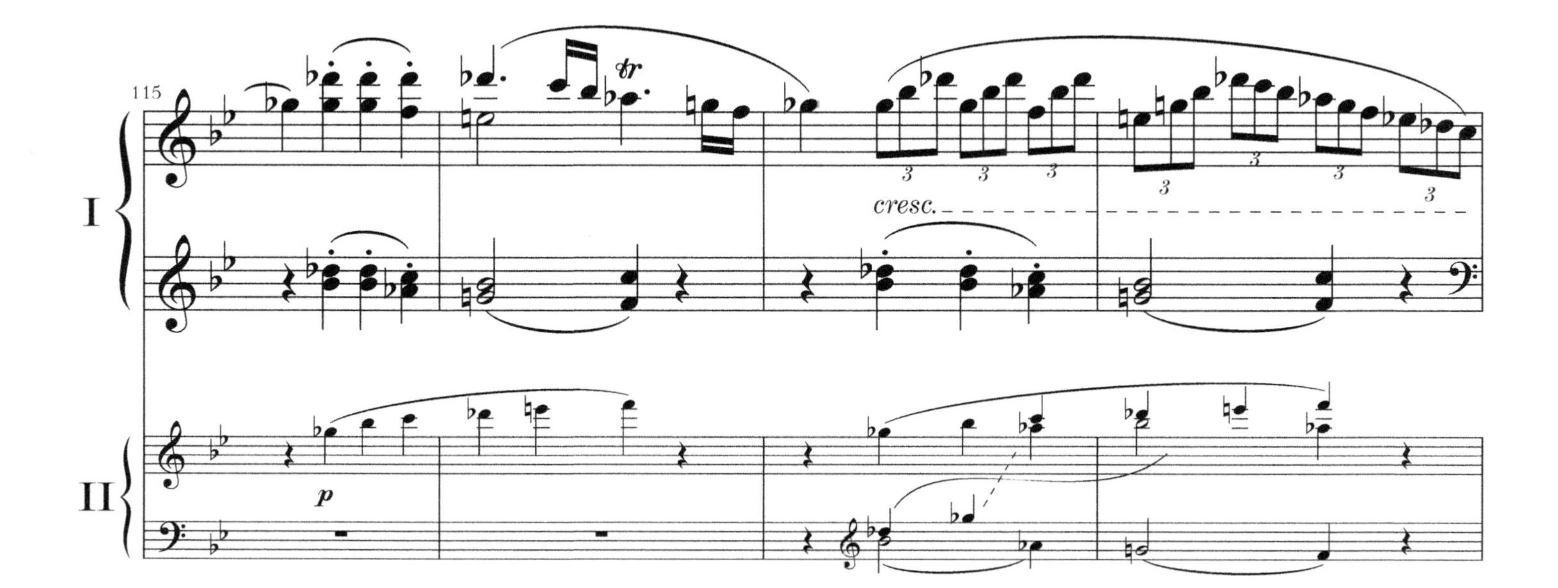
115
I
II
tr
cresc.
p

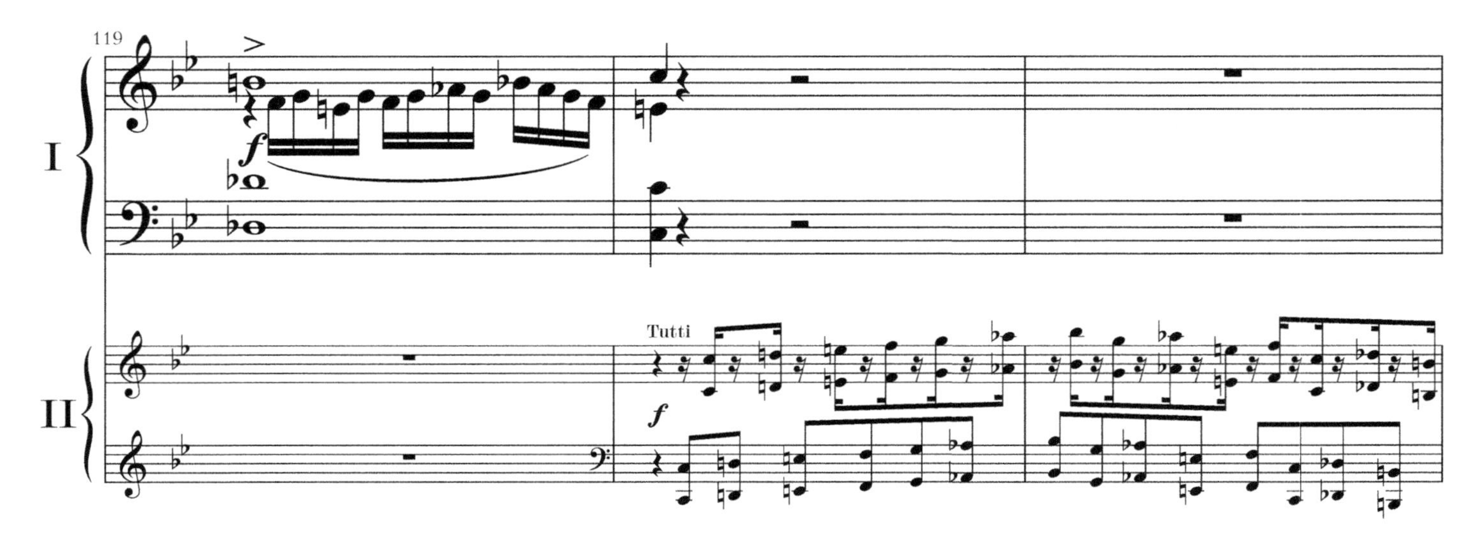
119
I
II
Tutti

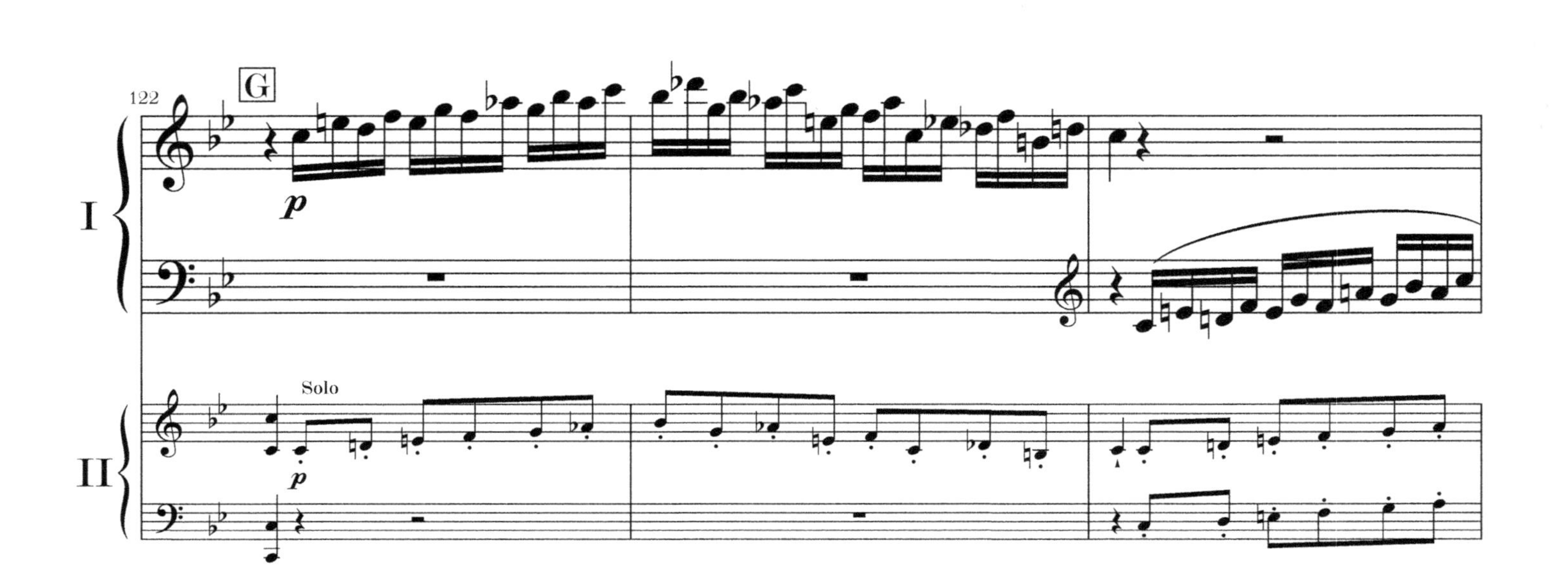
122
G
I
II
Solo

125
I
II

128
I
II
espr.
legato

131
I
II

135
I
II
p

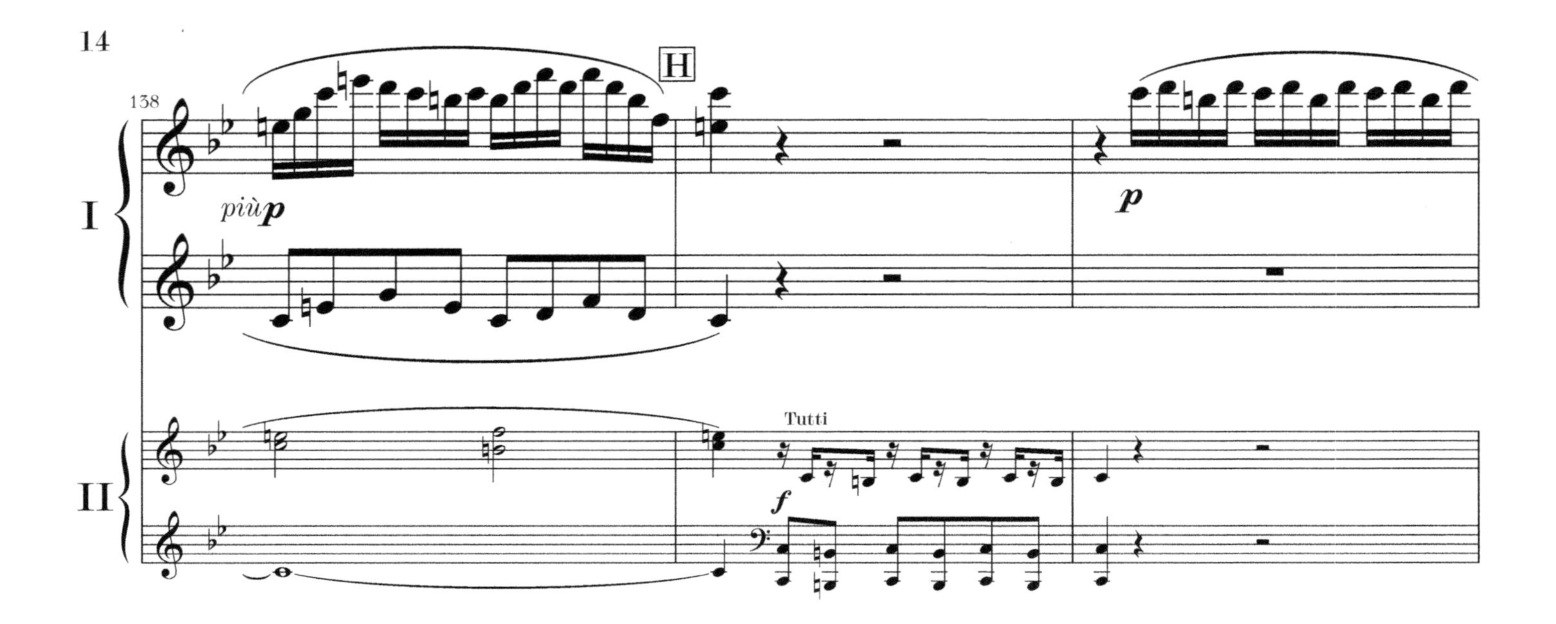
138
H
più p
I
Tutti
f
II
p

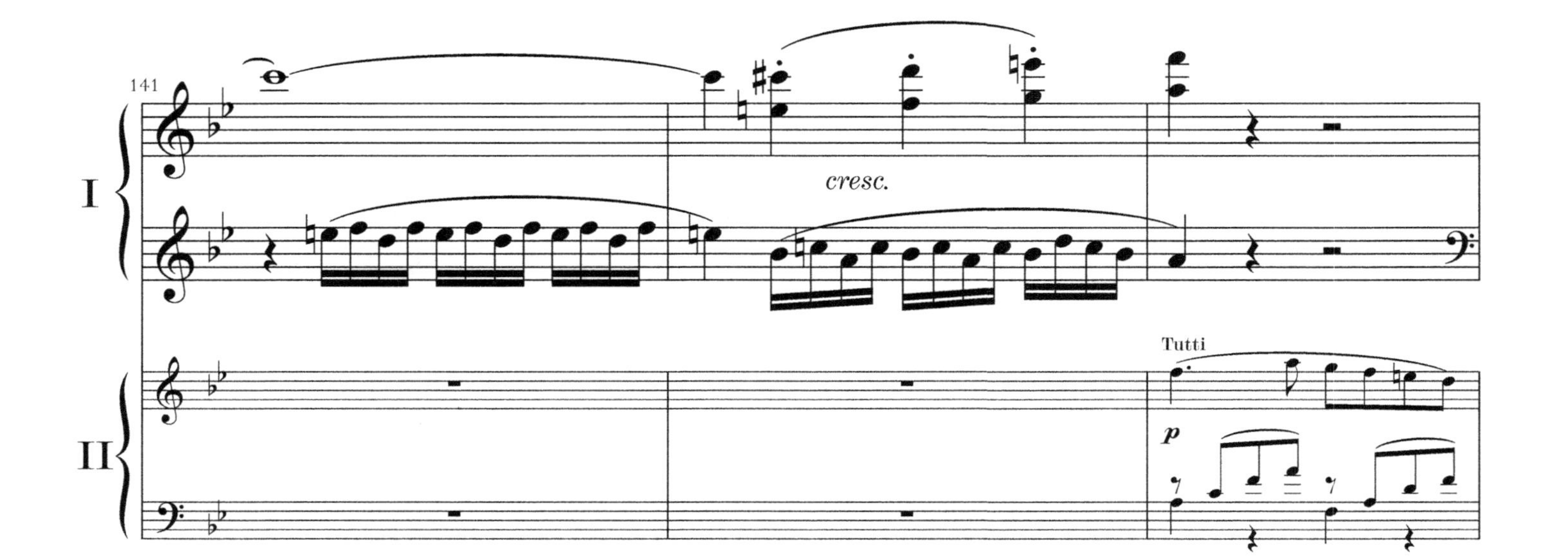
141
I
cresc.
Tutti
p
II

144
I
espr.
p
II
mf
p

148
I
II
mf
p

151
I
II
mf
p
pp
stacc.

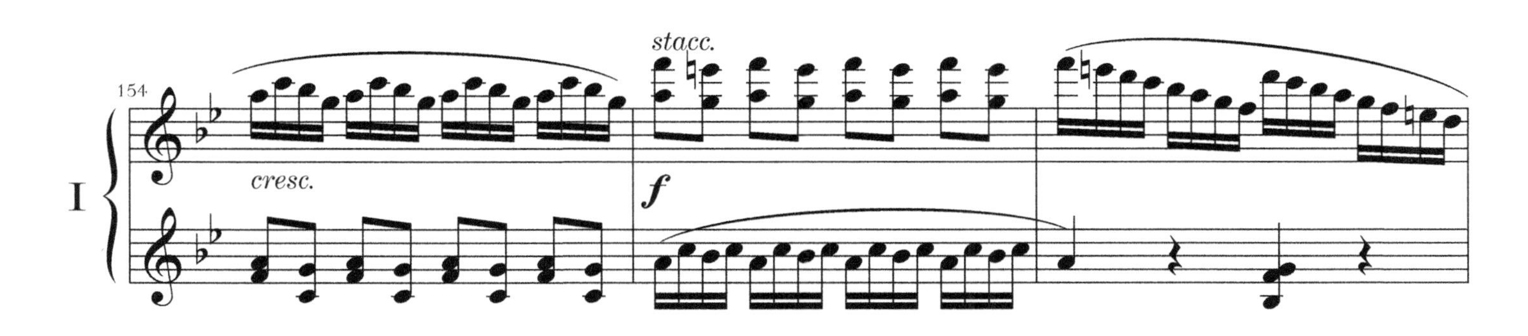
154
I
cresc.
stacc.
f

157
I
II
p
stacc.
cresc.

160
stacc.
f
I
p
II

163
I
p espr.
I
p
II

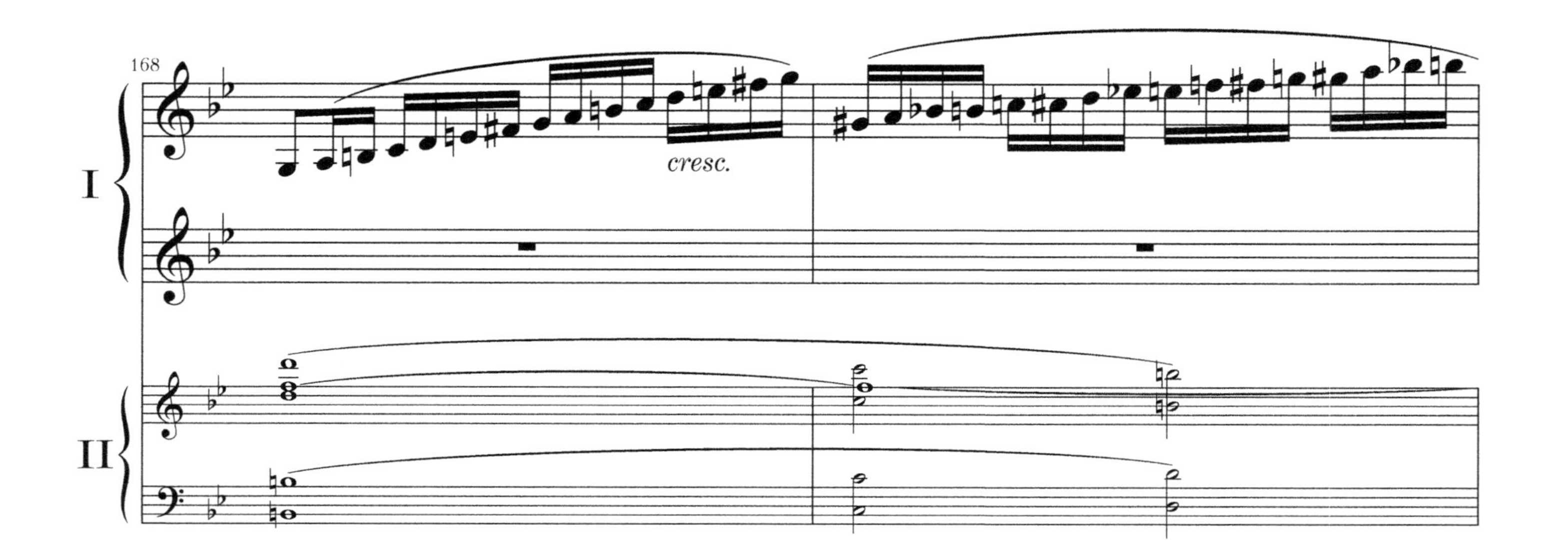
168
cresc.
I
II

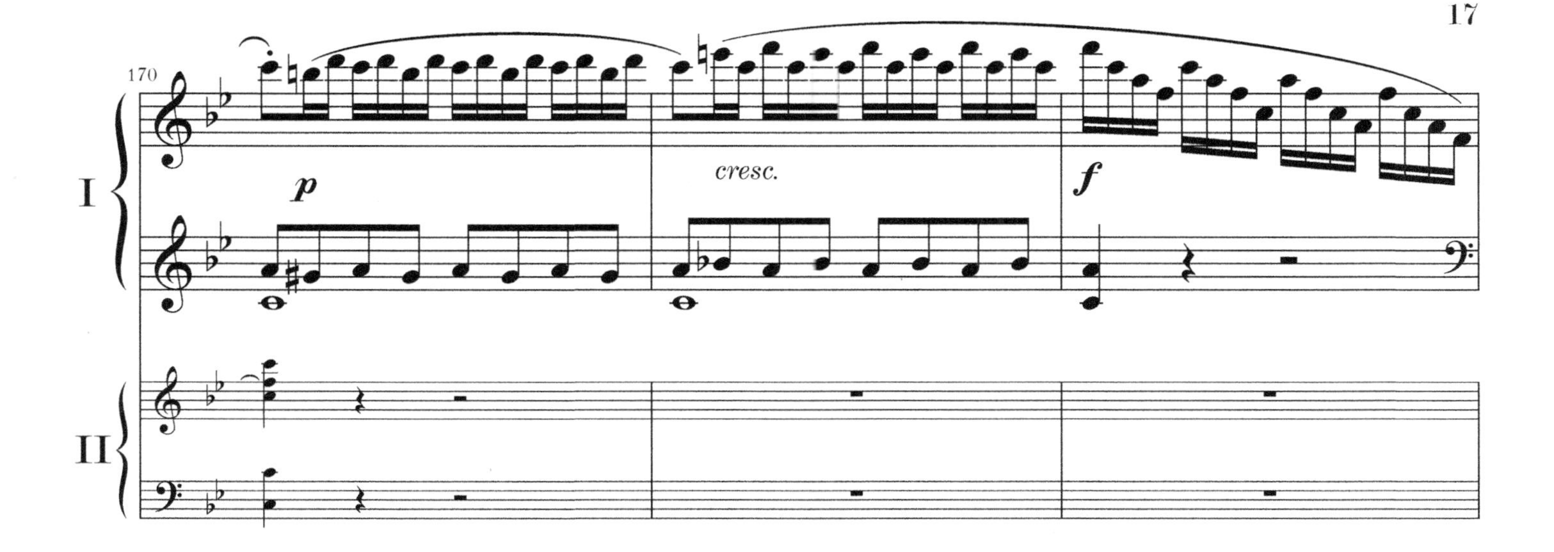
170
I
II
cresc.

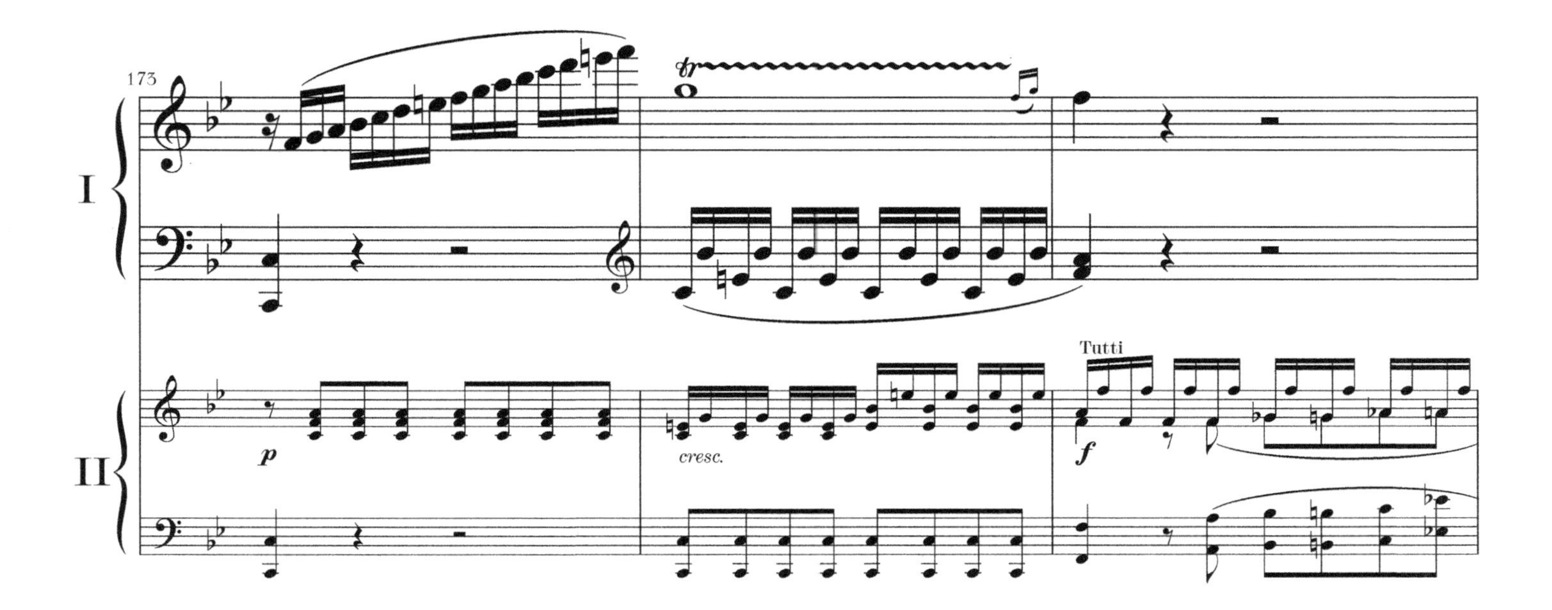
173
I
II
cresc.
Tutti

176
II

179
II

K
182
II
sf
p
sf

187
I
II
p
p

192
I
II
f

195
I
II
mf
p

199
I
II
p
f
p

203
I
II
Solo

207
L
p legato
I
II
p

210
I
II

213
cresc.
I
II

215
p
I
II

218
I
II
f
p
f
p

221
I
II
p
f
p

224
M
I
II
f

227
I
II

230
dim.
p
legato
I
II

233
p
I
II

237
I
3
3
cresc.
II

240
I
N
II
Tutti
p

243
II
f
p

247
II
f
p

251
II
f

255
I
II
f
p
Solo
p

258
I
II
legato

261
I
II

264
I
II
cresc.
Tutti
p
f

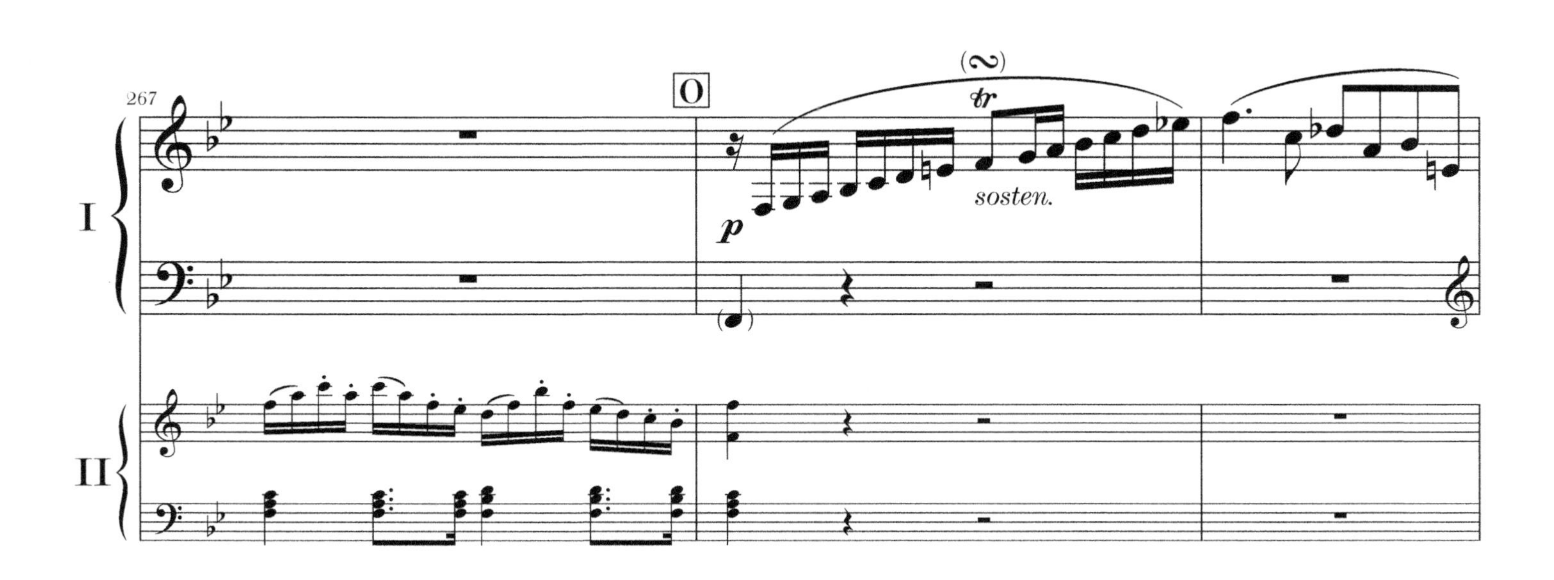
267
O
I
II
(∾)
tr
p
sosten.

270
I
II
mf
Solo
p

273
I
II
p

277
I
II
cresc.

281
I
II
f
Tutti
f

284
I
II
Solo
p

287
I
II

290
P
legato
I
II

293
I
II

296
I
II

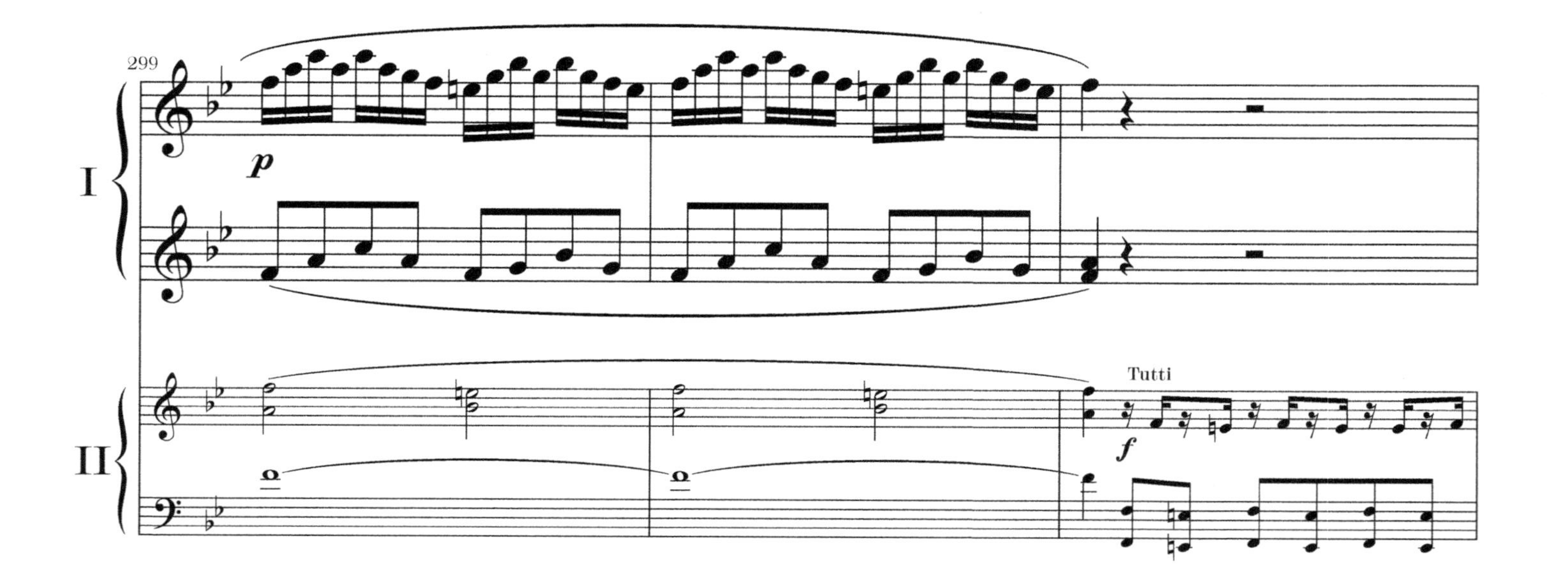
299
I
II
Tutti

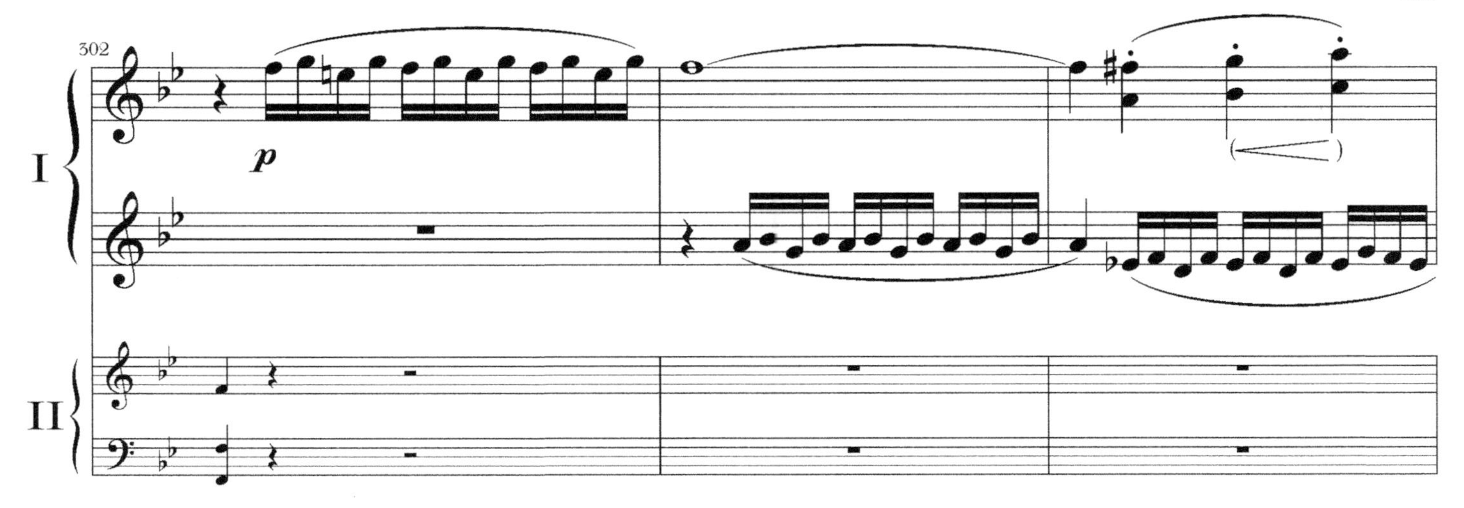
302
I
II
p

305
I
II
Tutti
p
mf
p

309
I
II
p espr.
mf
p
Solo
mf
p

312
I
II
mf
p
mf
p

315
I
II
stacc.
pp
stacc.
cresc.
f

318
I
II
p
stacc.
p

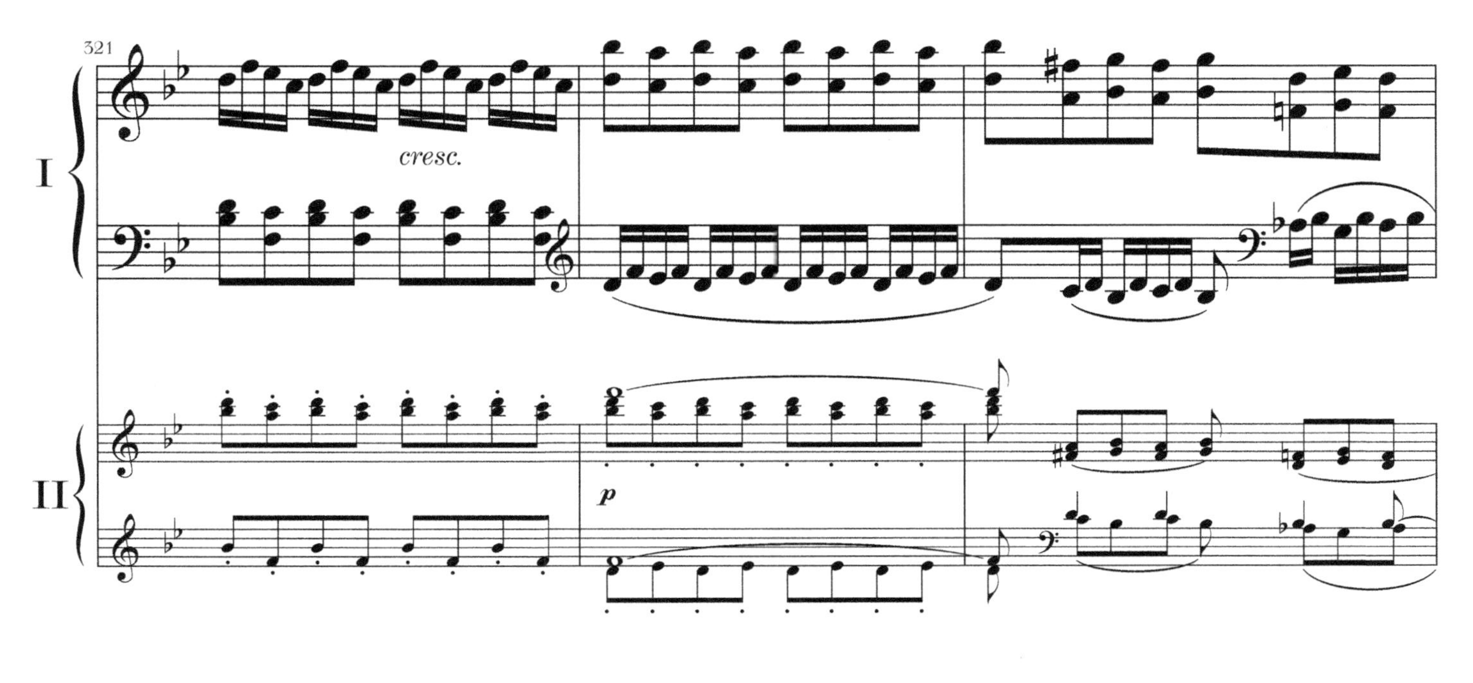
321
I
II
cresc.
p

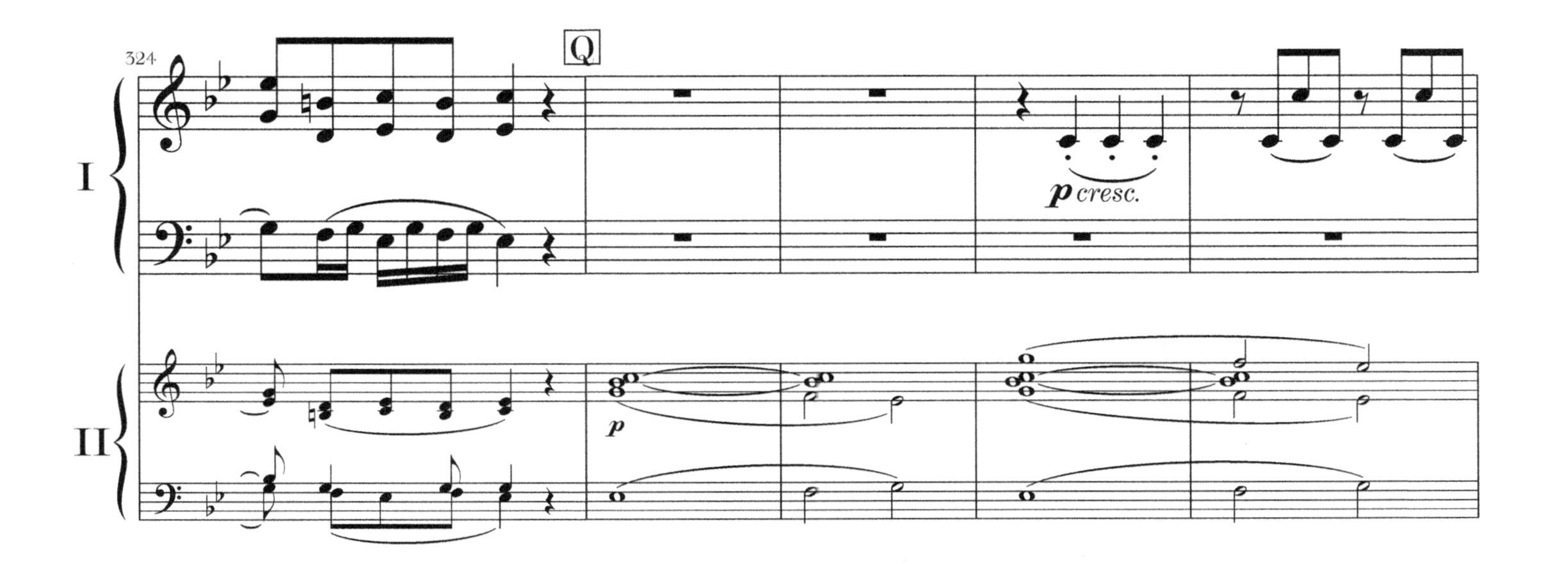
324
Q
I
II
p cresc.
p

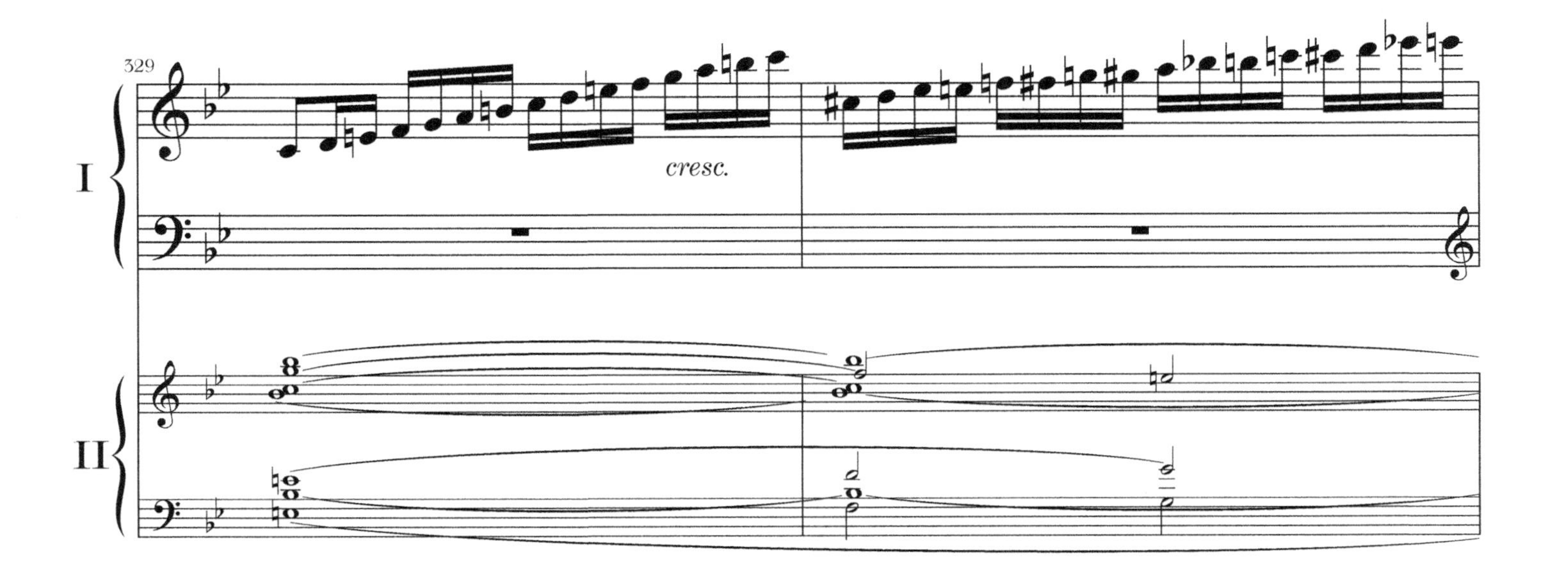
329
I
II
cresc.

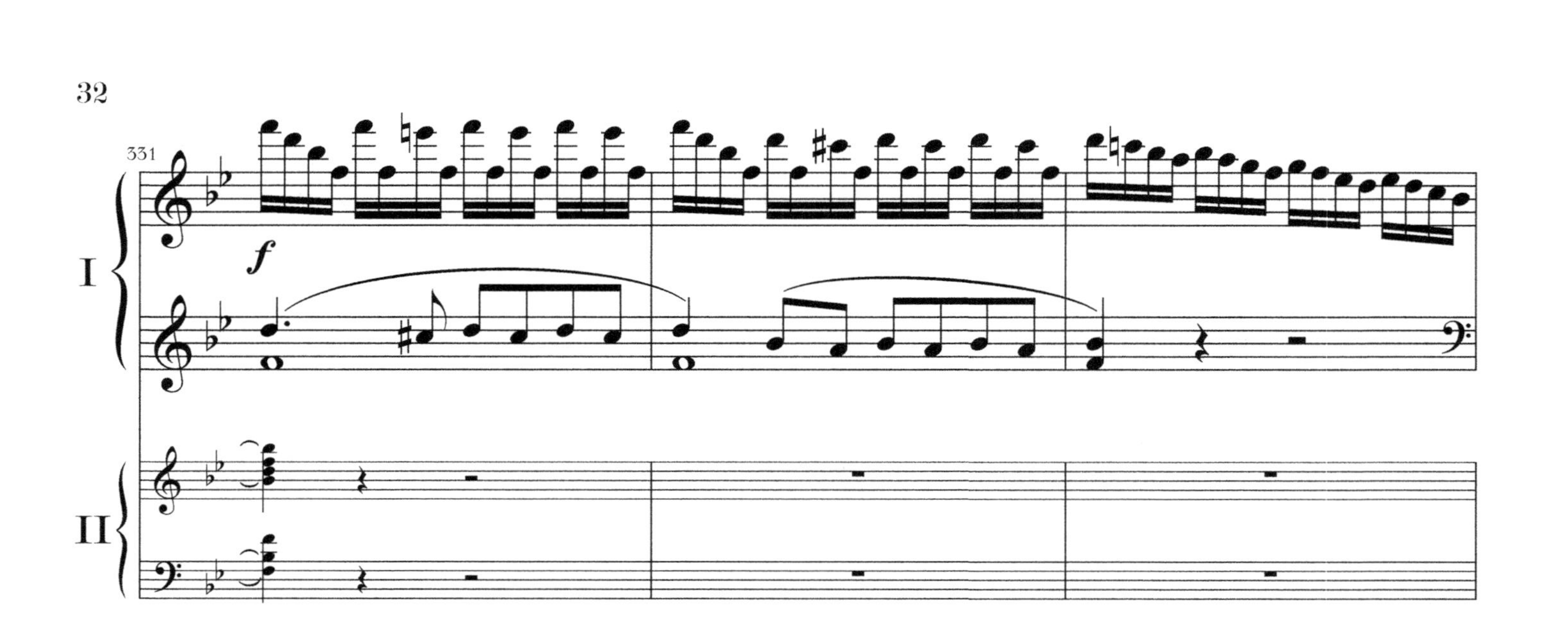
331
I
II

334
I
Tutti
II

339
I
II

344
I
II
Solo
p
mf

348
I
II

R
352
I
II
Tutti
f

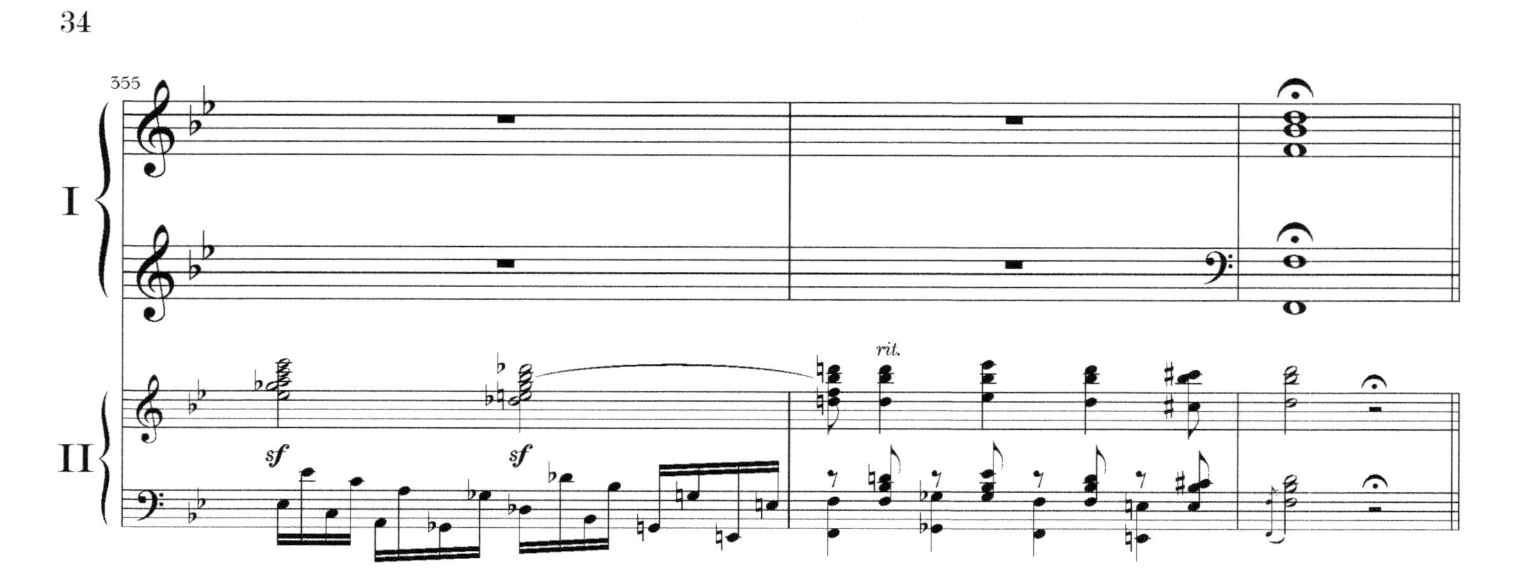

Cadenza by W.A.Mozart

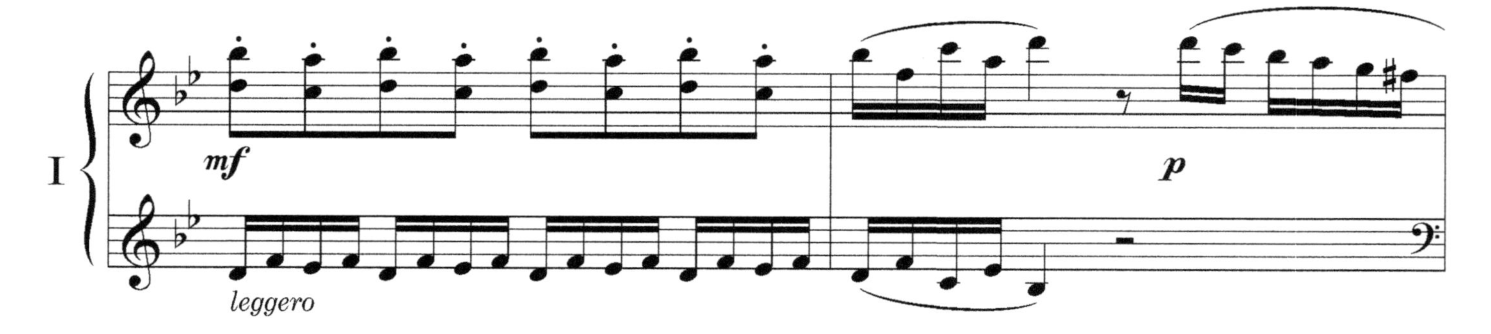

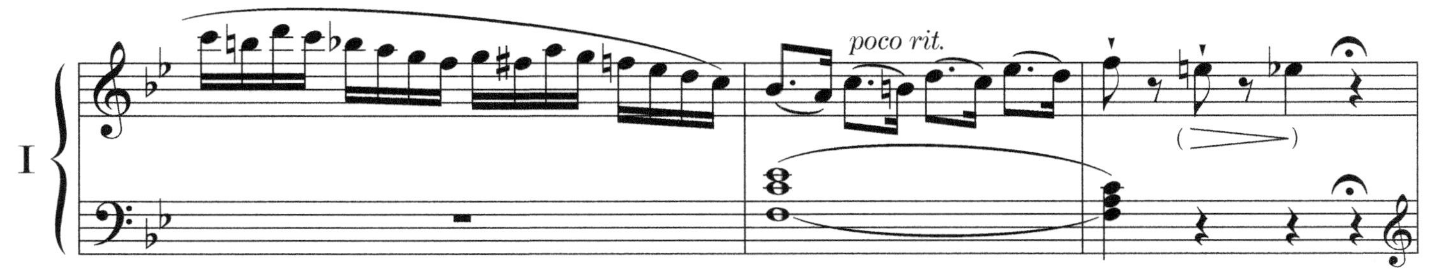
I
poco rit.

I
a tempo
p
espr.
legato
pp
p
una corda
Ped.

I
pp
p

I
rit.
sf
Ped.

I
f
5
a tempo
dim.
p
rit.
Ped.

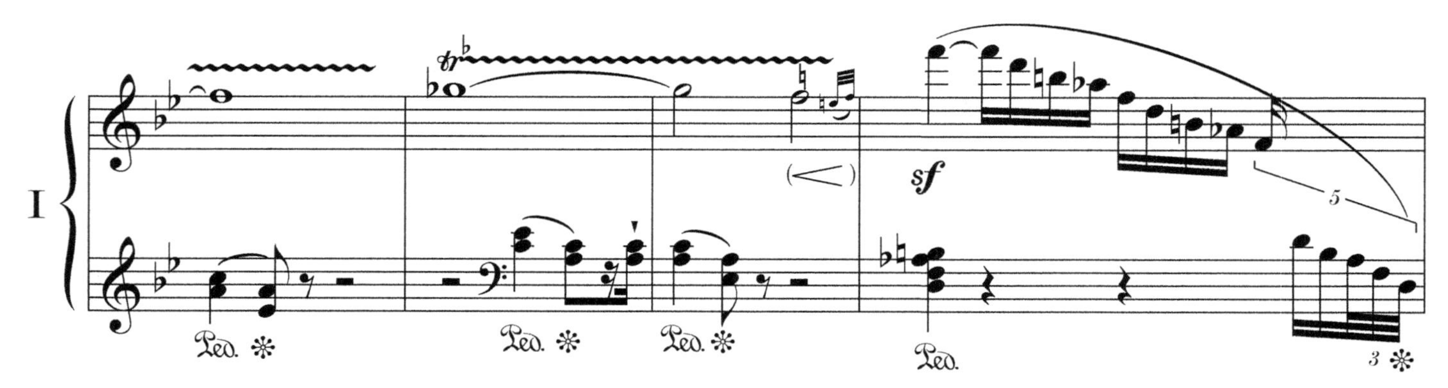
I
Ped.

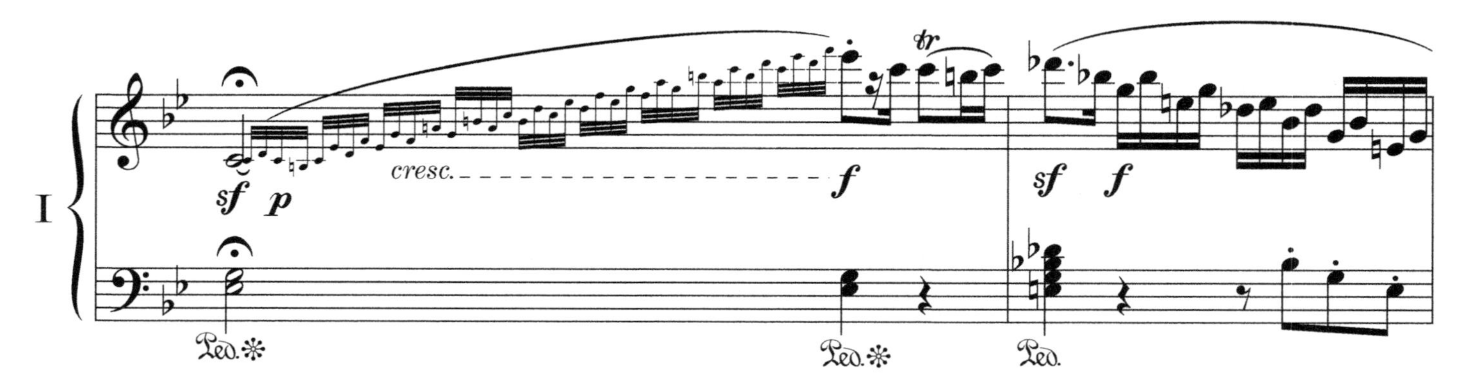
I
cresc.
Ped.

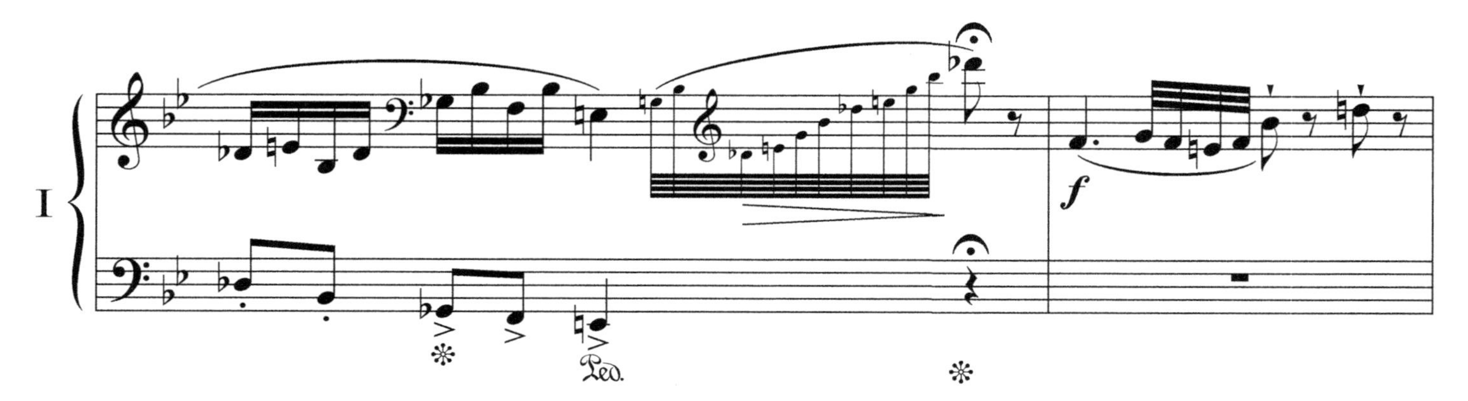
I
Ped.

tranquillo
I

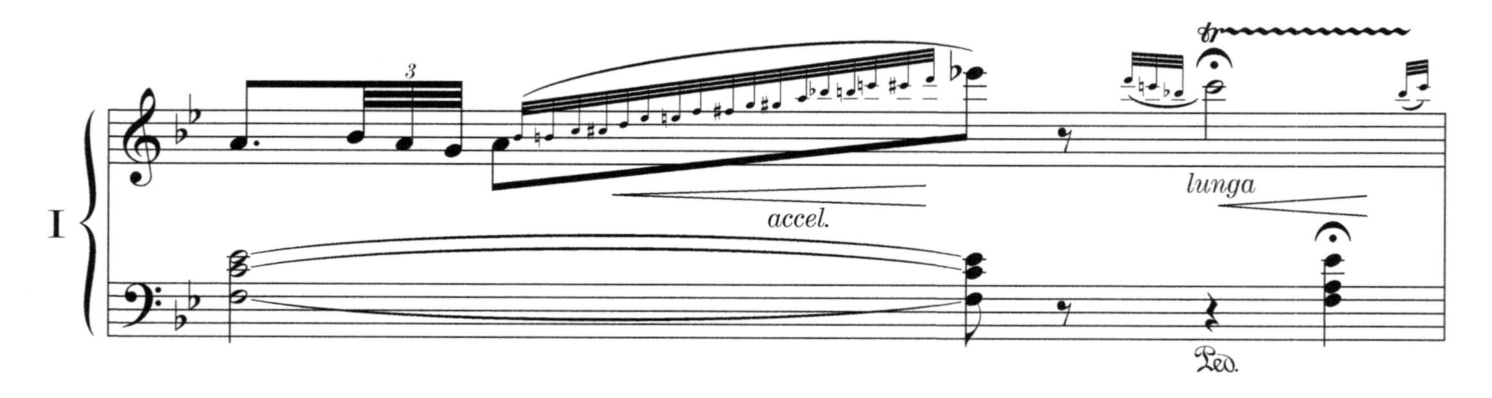
I
accel.
lunga
Ped.

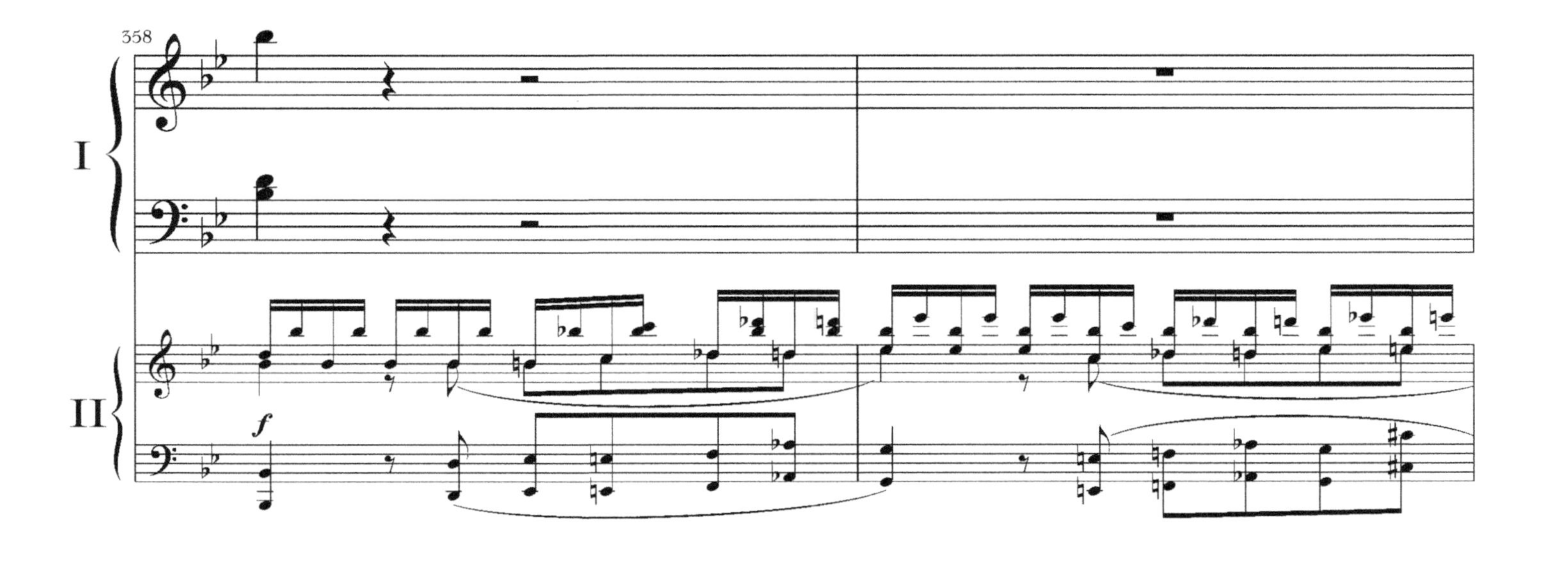
358
I
II
f

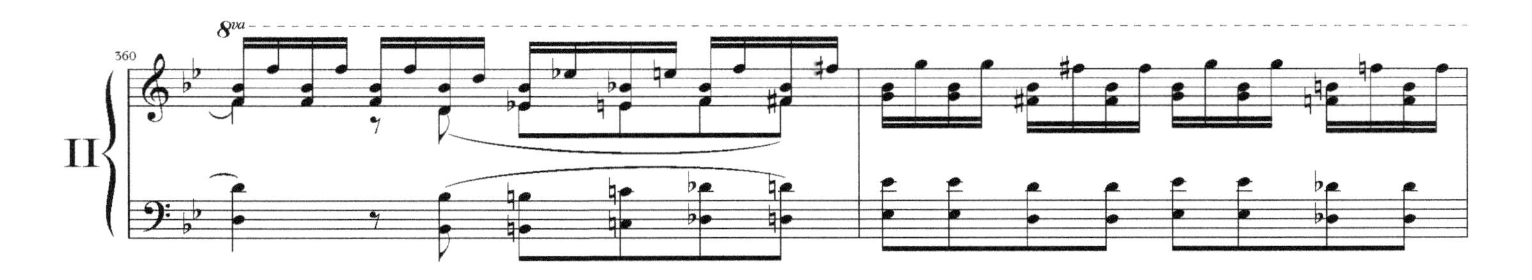
360
8va
II

362
(8va)
tr
II
Ped.

364
II
p

367
II
p

II

One measure of taps precedes music

16
A
I
II
mf
con Ped.

20
I
p
cresc.

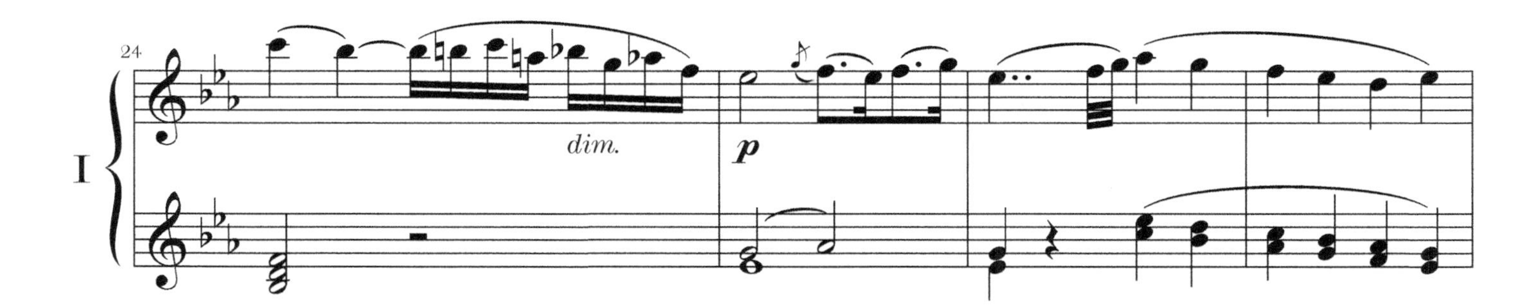
24
I
dim.
p

28
I
II
p

33
II
f
tr

36
II
tr
B
p

39
II
tr
Ped.

42
II
tr

45
II

48
C
I
II
p molto espressivo
p

52
I
II

56
I
II

60
I
II
più mf
p

64
D
I
II
p
dolce
l.h.

67
I
II

71
I
II
3
f
mf

75
I
II
p

78
I
II
pp
con Ped.

82
E
I
II
p

86
I
II
p

90
I
II
mf

94
I
II
p
cresc.

97
I
II
mf
p
più p
cresc.

100
I
II
sf
p
ad lib.
cresc.
dim.

F
103
I
mf
II
p

107
I
II

111
r.h.
l.h.
I
Tutti
II
f

114
II
tr
tr

116
II
p

118
I
mp
II
tr

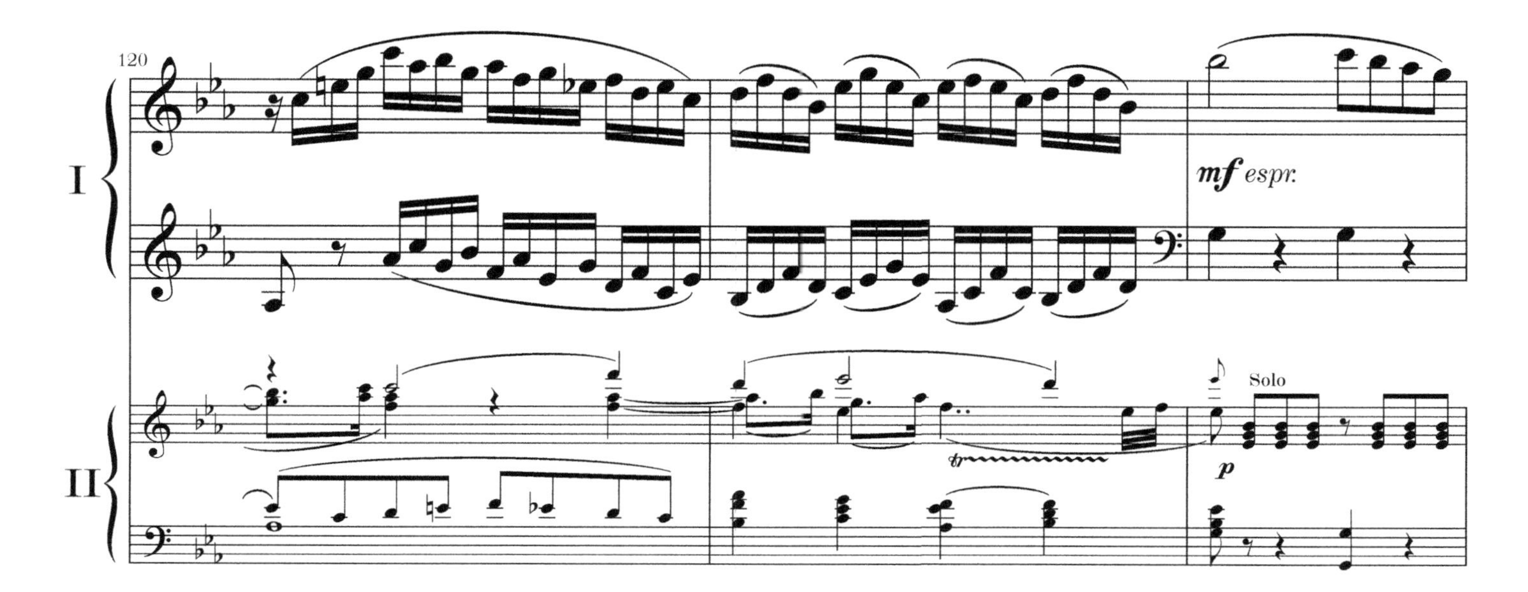
120
I
mf espr.
II
tr
Solo
p

123
I
II

126
I
II
mf
l.h.

129
I
II
p

III

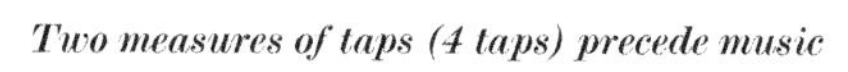
Two measures of taps (4 taps) precede music

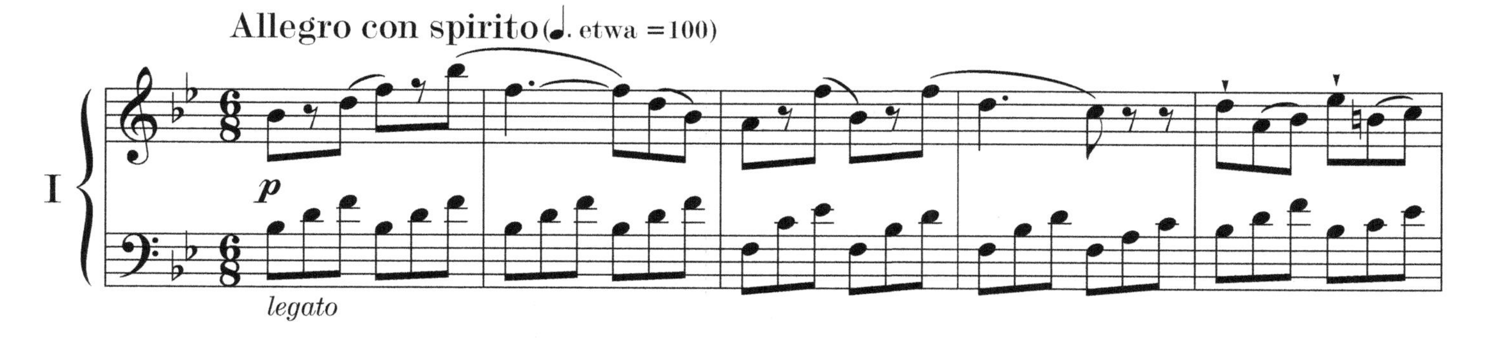
Allegro con spirito (♩. etwa =100)
I
p
legato

6
I

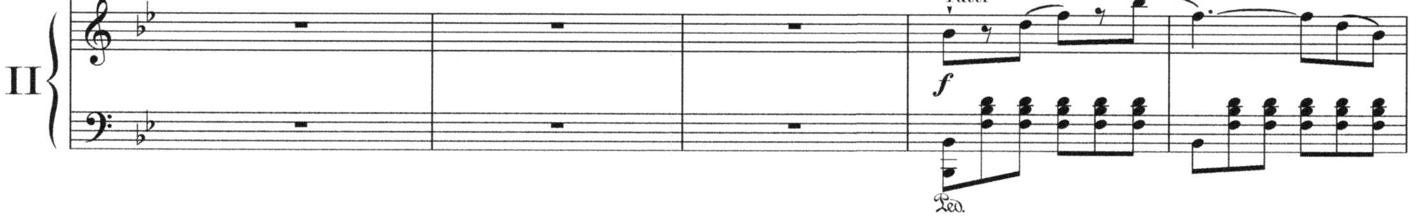
II
Tutti
f
Ped.

11
II

16
I
p
(legato)
II

21
I

26
I

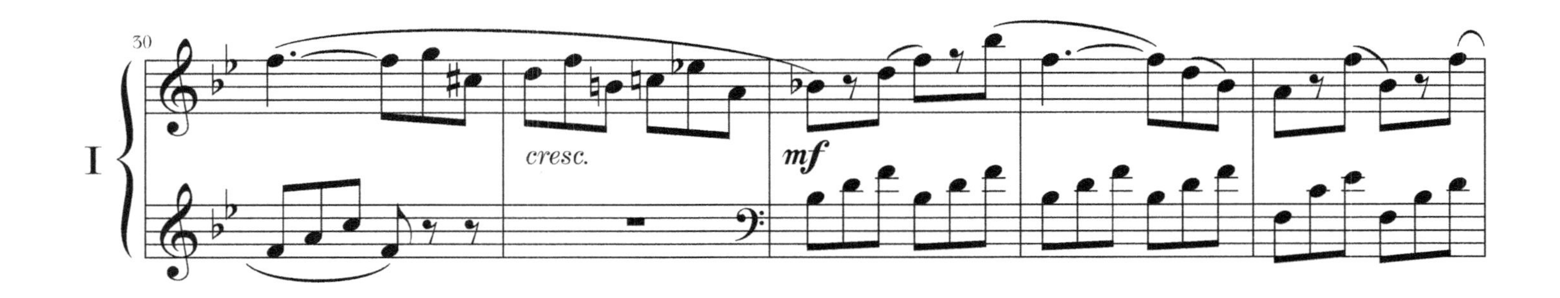
30
I
cresc.
mf

35
I

A
Tutti
40
II
f
p

45
II
f
p

50
II
f

54
II

57
II
p

61
B
I
p
II

67
I
mf
II
Solo
p

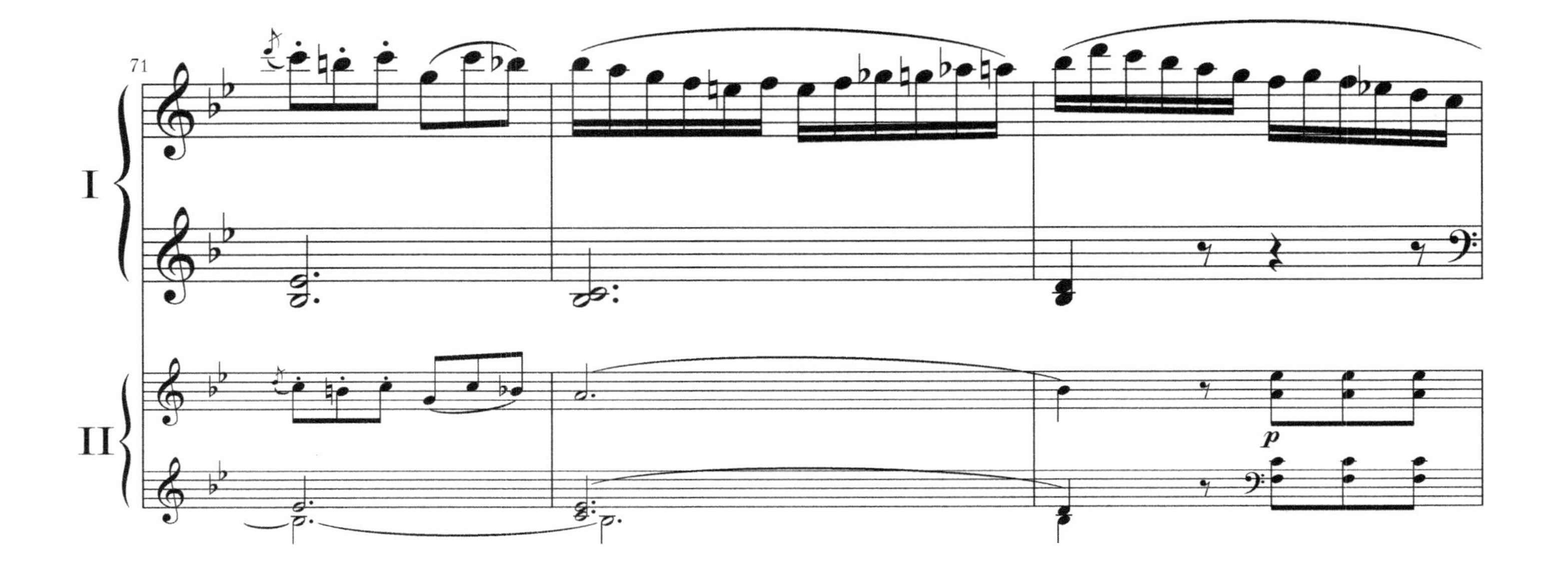
71
I
II
p

74
I
p
cresc.
II

77
C
I
II

81
I
II

85
I
II

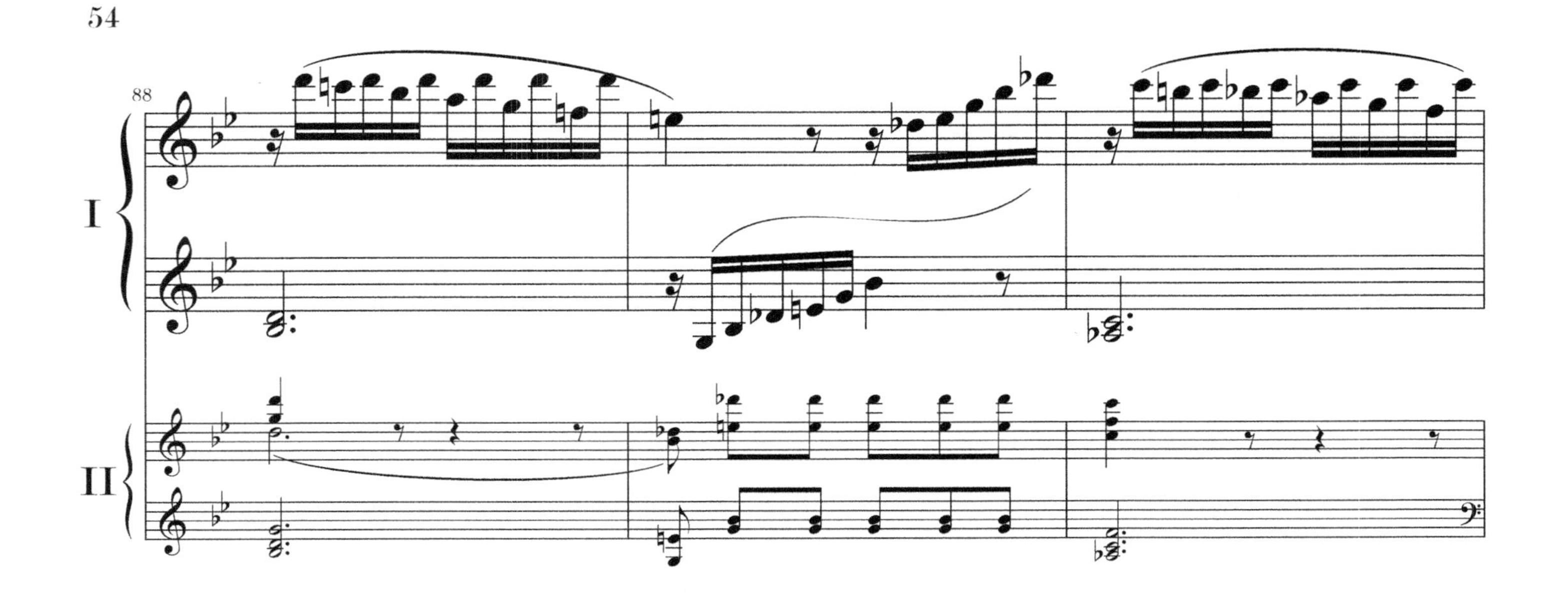
88
I
II

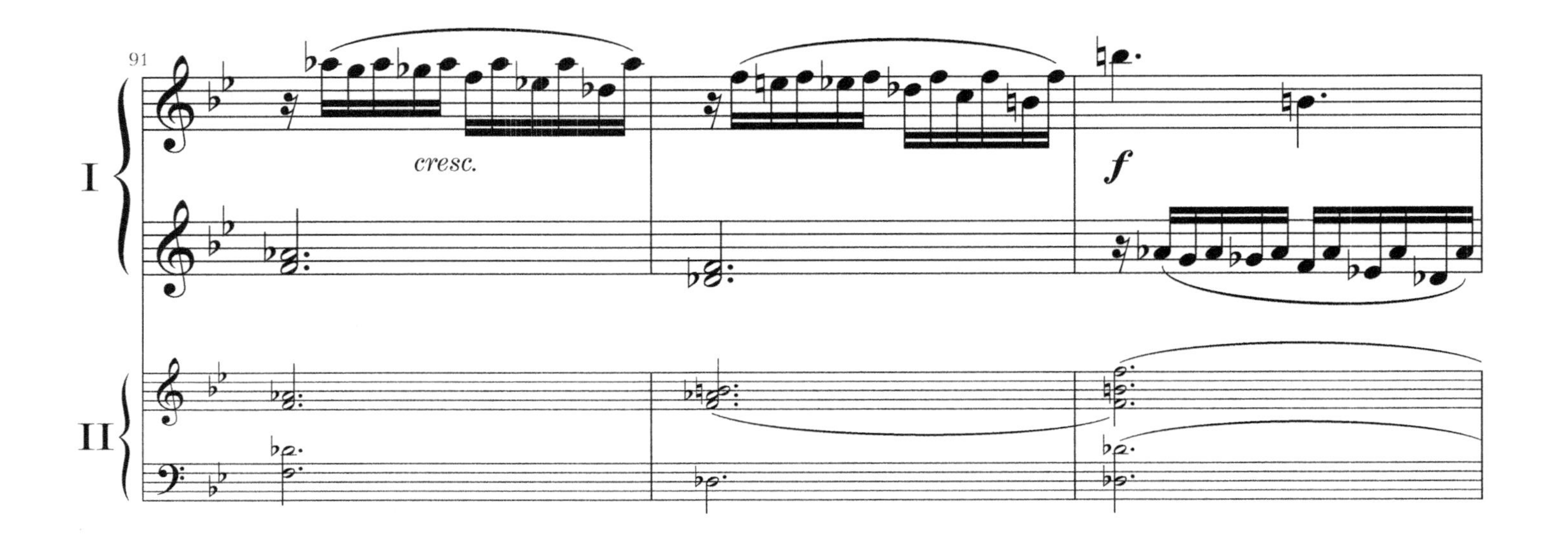
91
I
cresc.
f
II

94
I
legato
D
II
Tutti
f

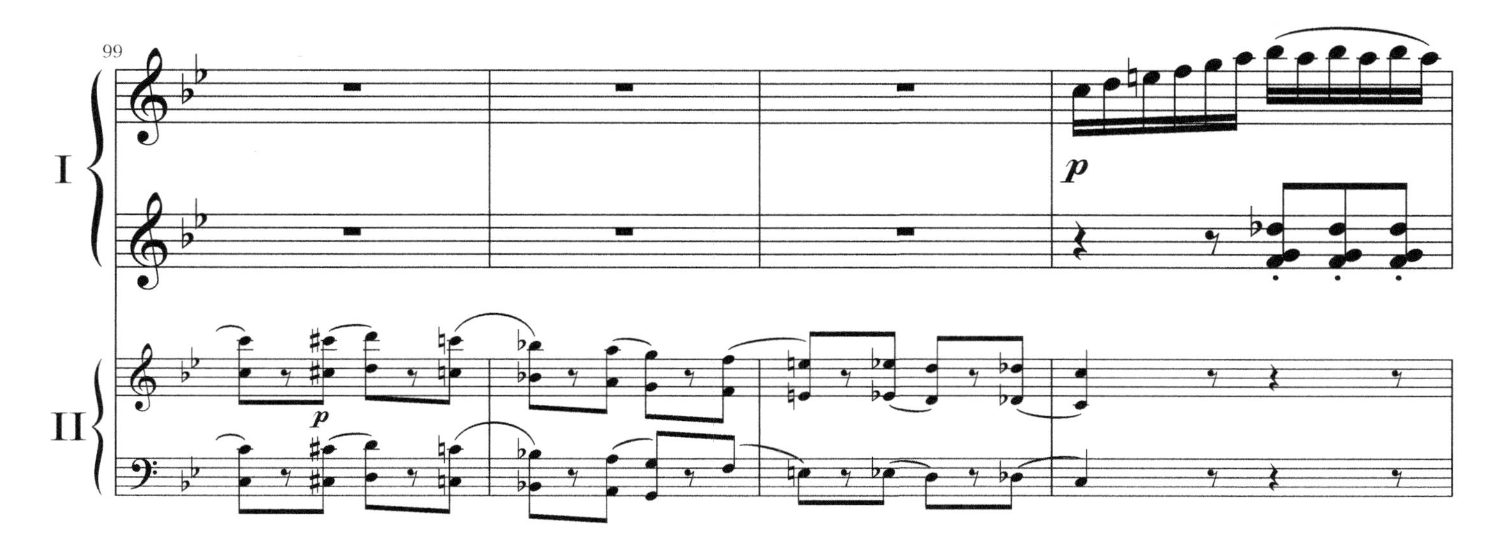
99
I
II
p
p

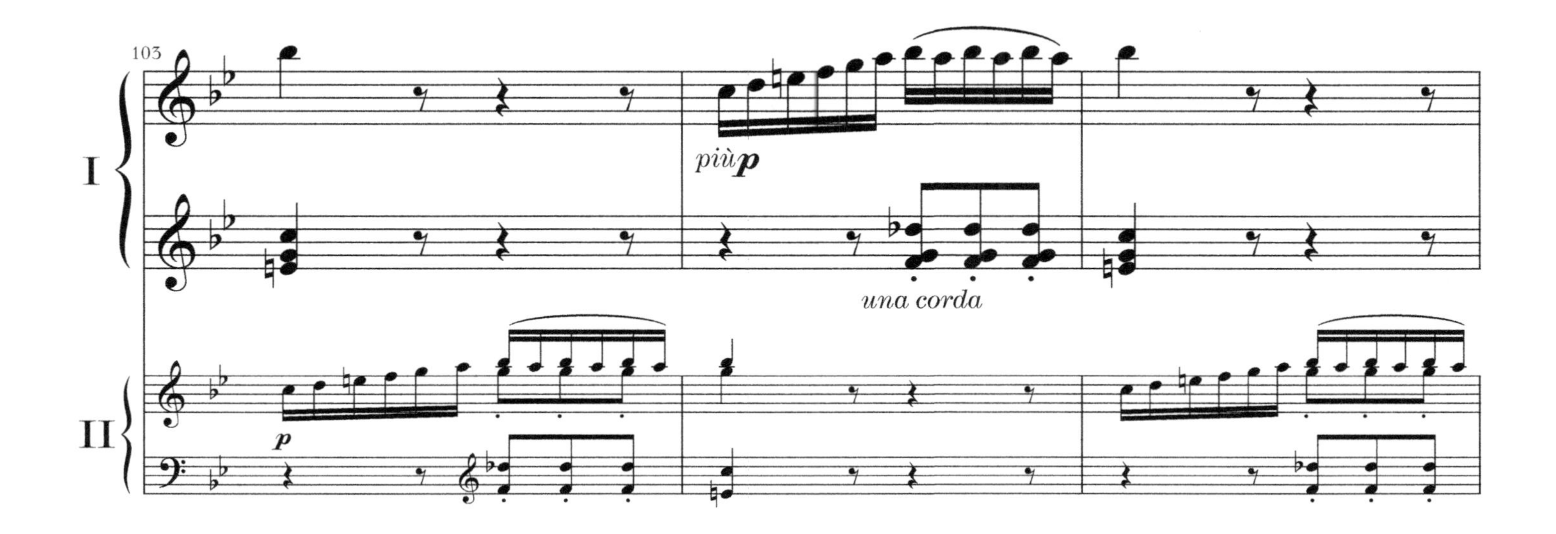
103
I
II
p
più p
una corda

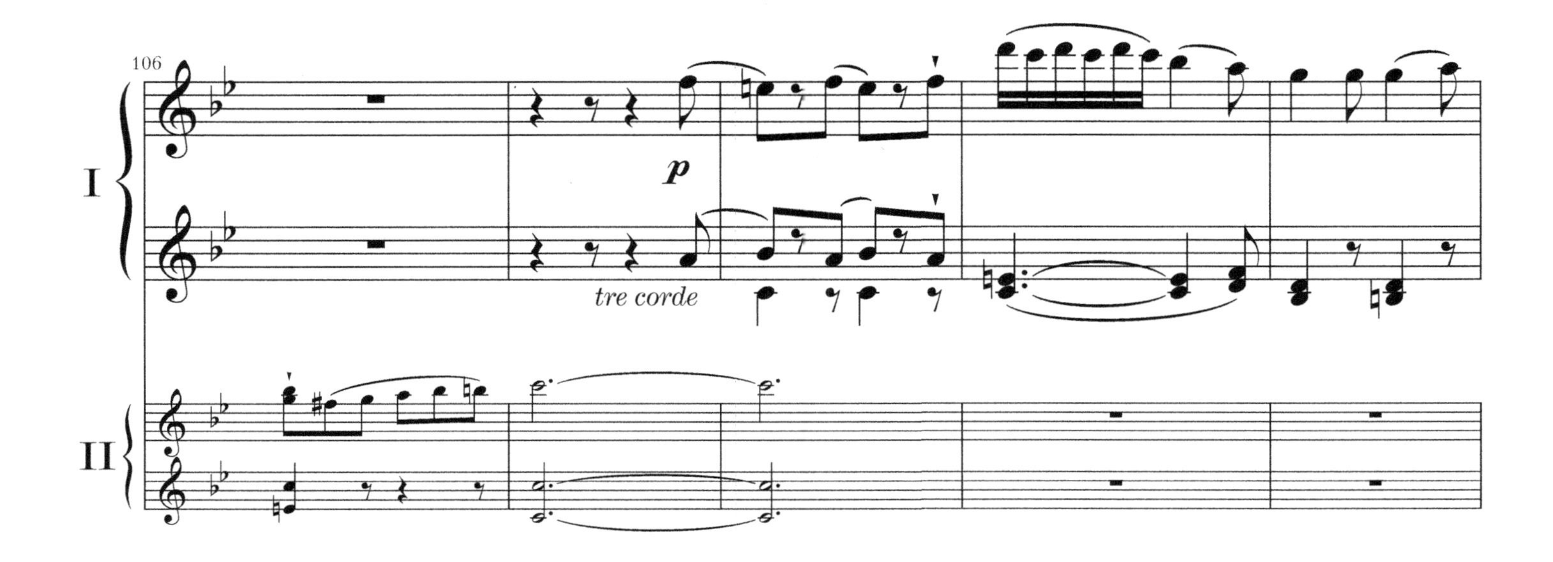
106
I
II
p
tre corde

111
I
II
p

116
I
II

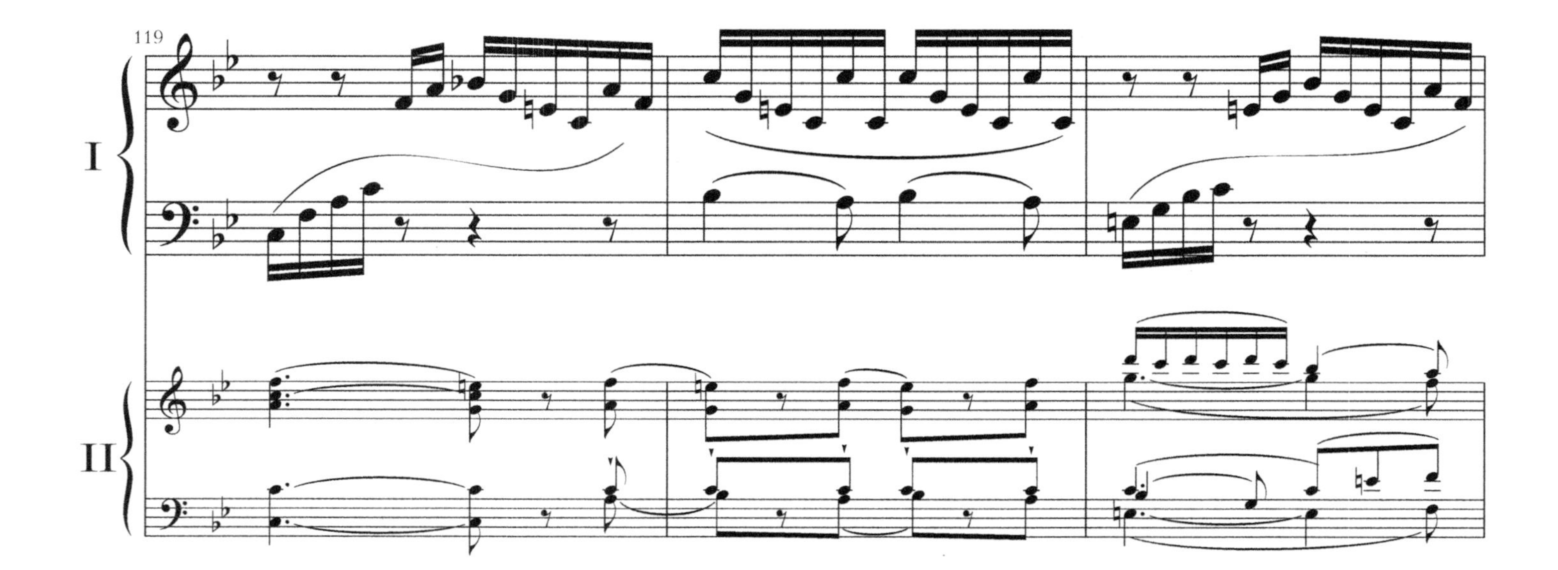
119
I
II

122
E
I
II
p

125
cresc.
I
II

127
più cresc.
I
p
II
cresc.

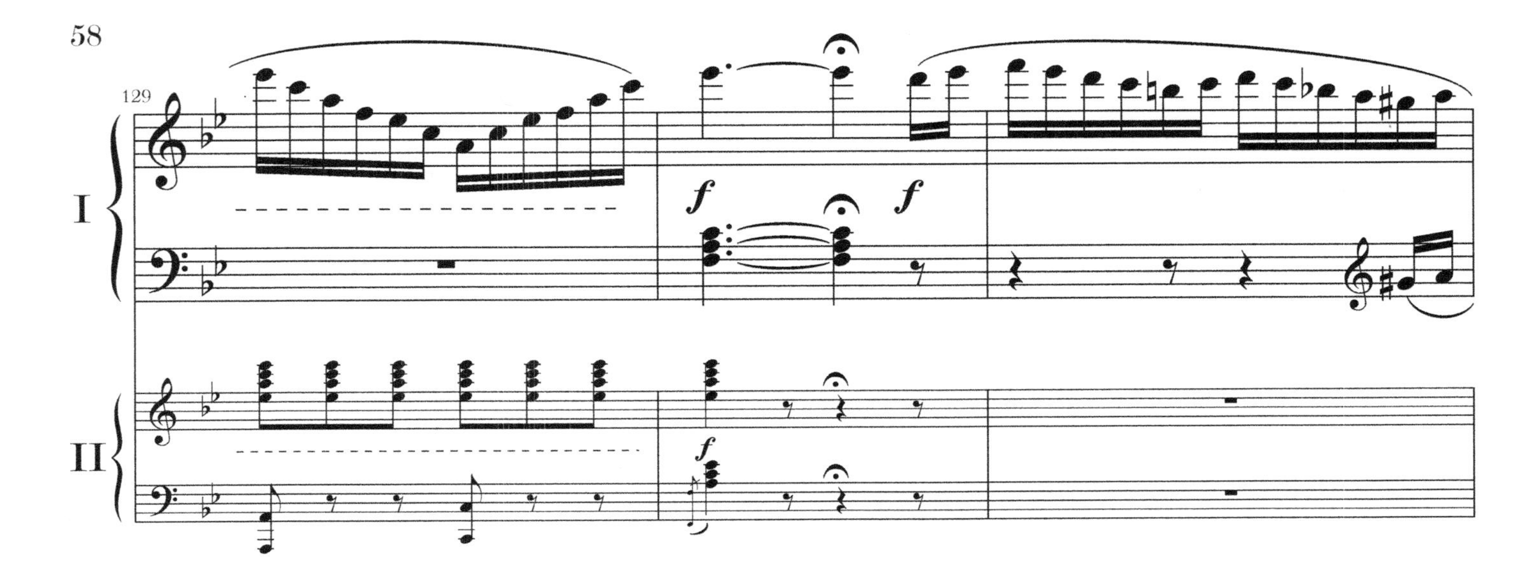
129
I
II
f
f
f

I

I
legato
Ped.
Ped.
Ped.
Ped.
Ped.

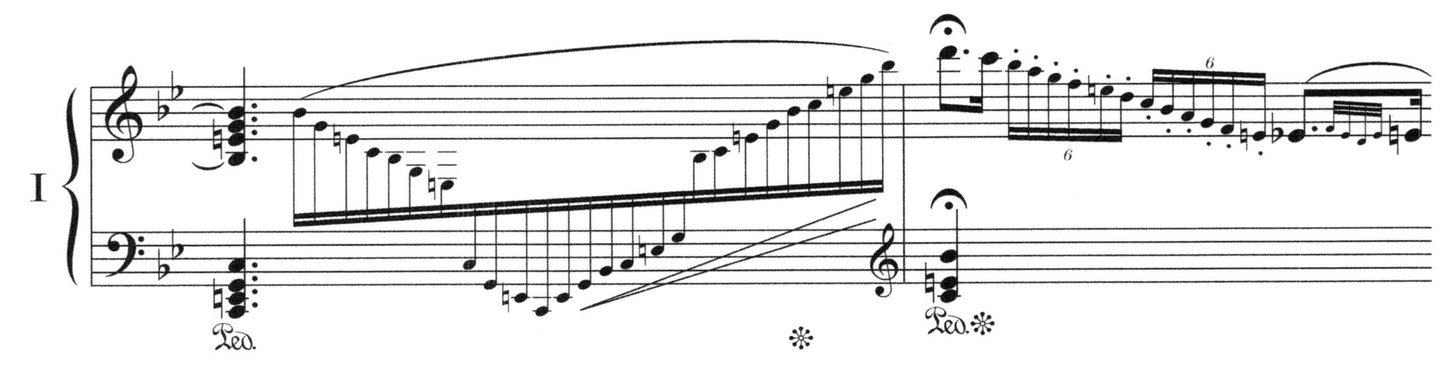
I
6
6
Ped.
Ped.

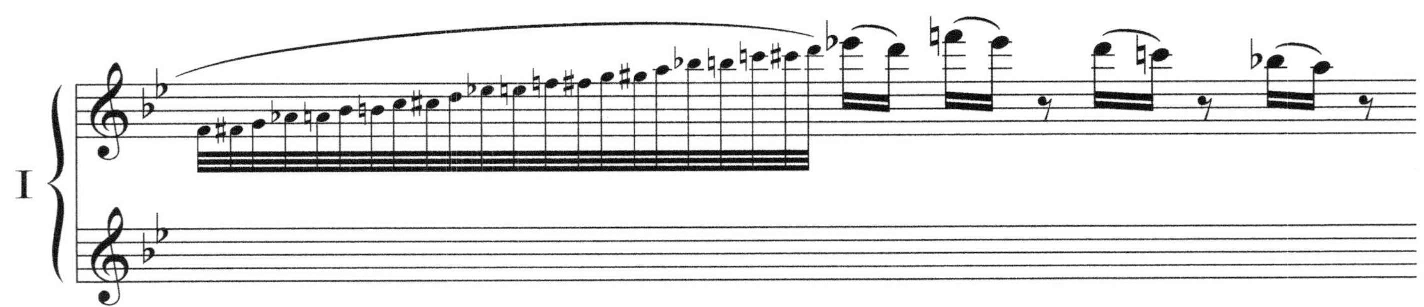
I

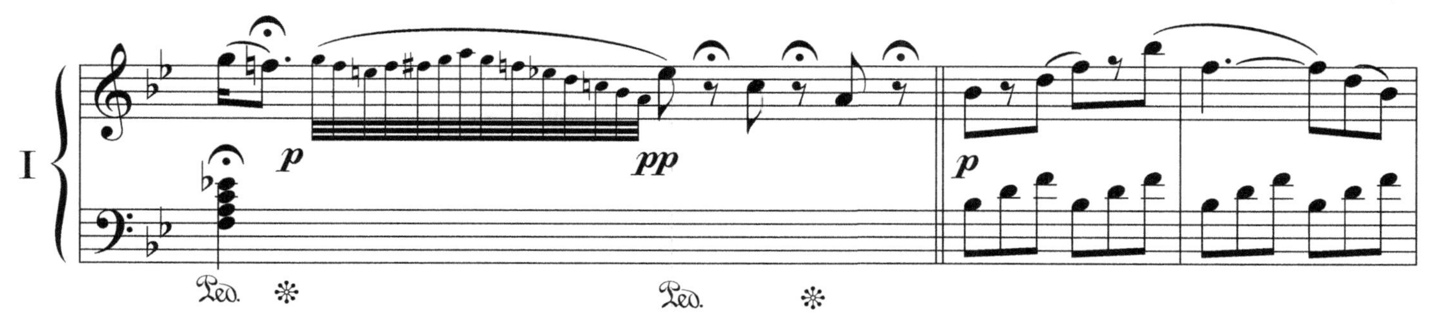
I
p
pp
p

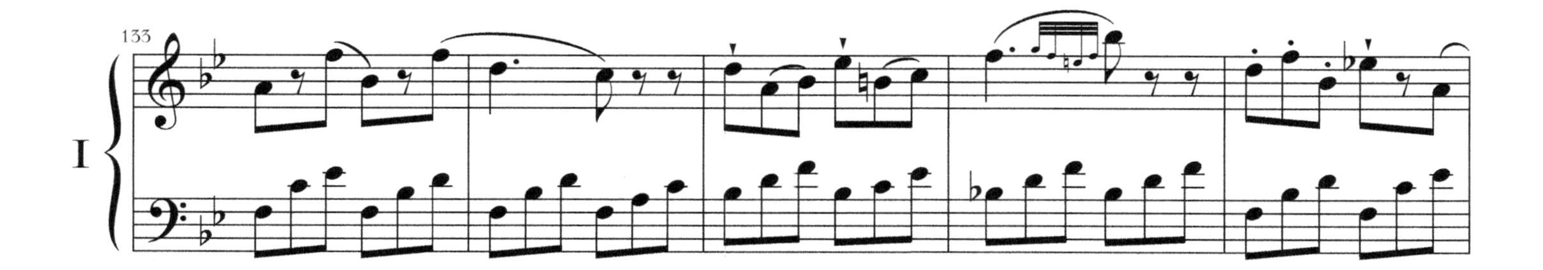
133
I

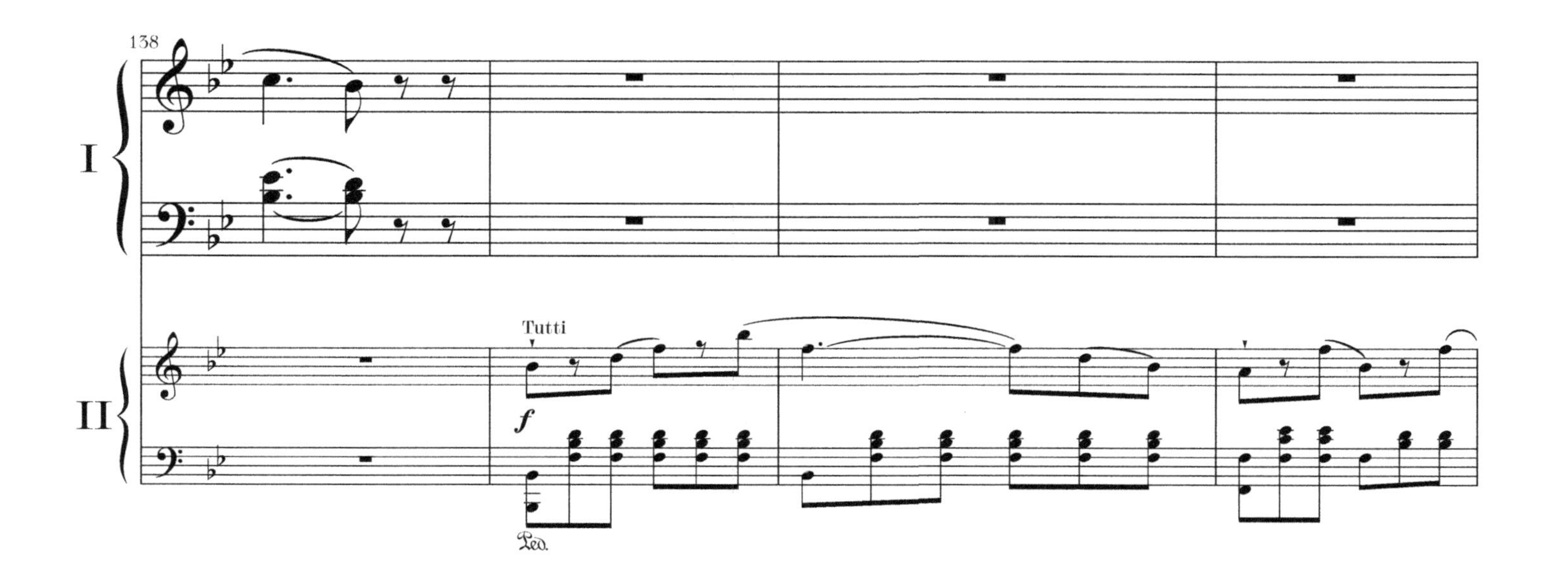
138
I
II
Tutti
f

142
II
p

quasi Cadenza
146
I
II
p
mf

150
I
f
dim.

154
I
cresc.

156
I
f

159
I
cresc.
f

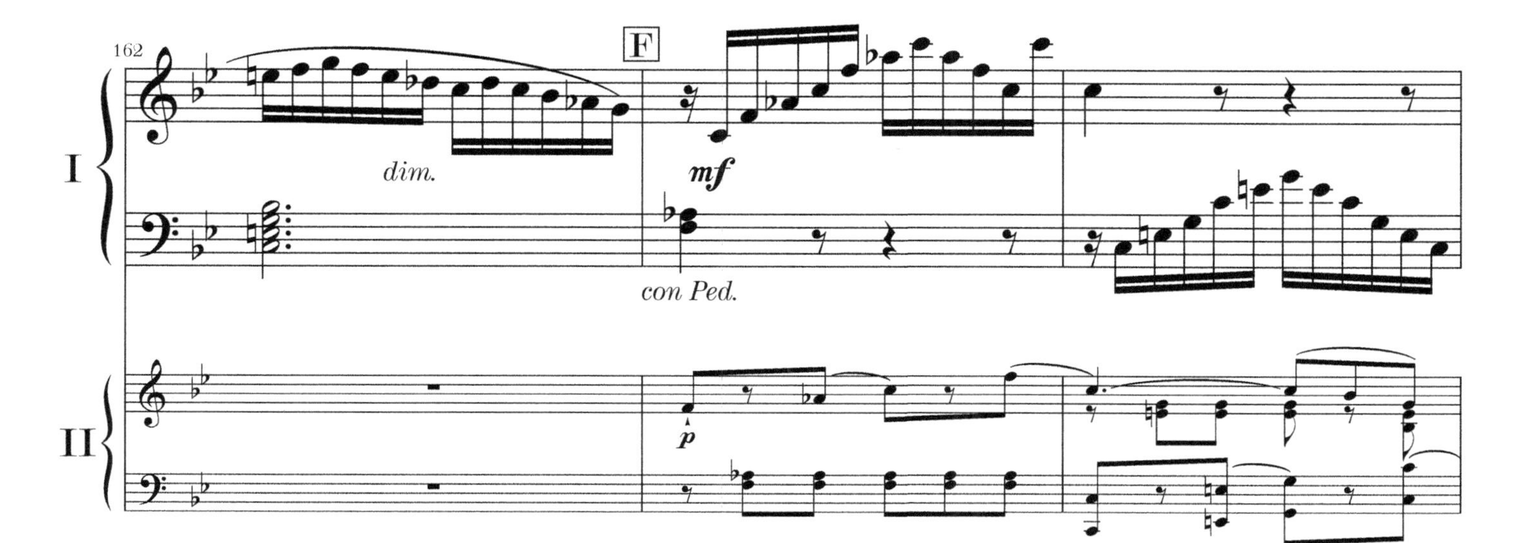
162
F
I
dim.
mf
con Ped.
II
p

165
I
cresc.
II

168
I
II

171
I
II

174
I
f
II

Cadenza
177
I
ff rit.
f
assai presto
f
II
f

I

I
rall.

182
G
I
p

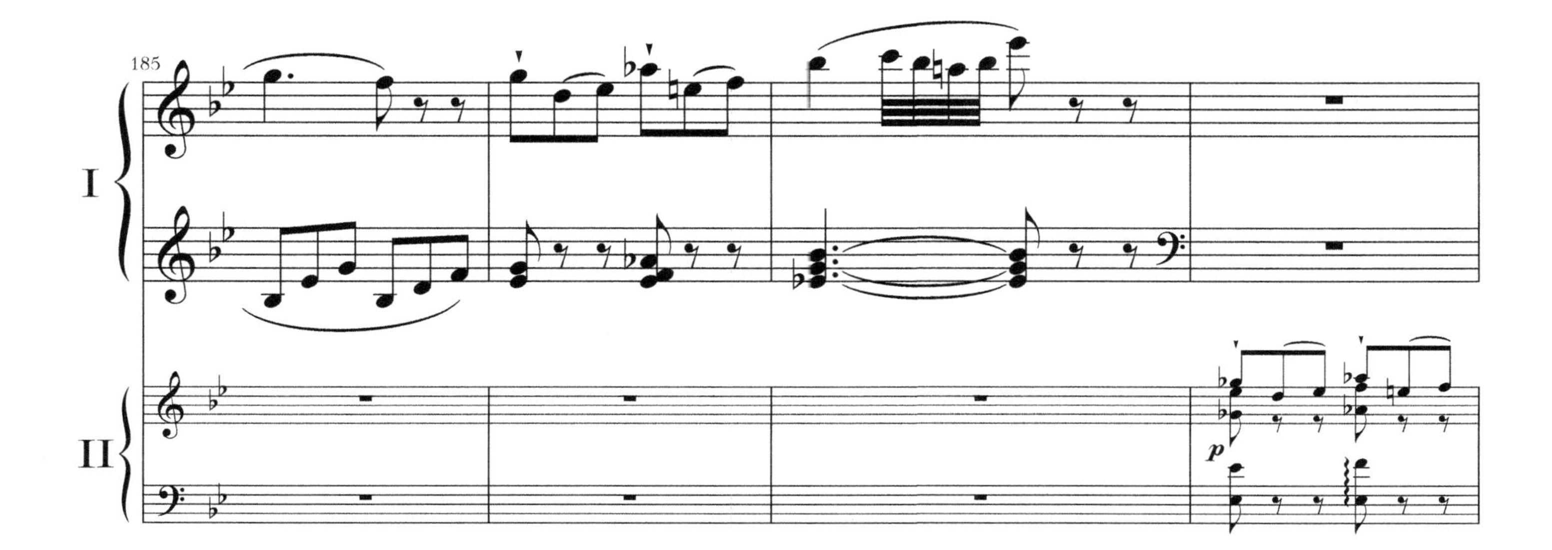
185
I
II
p

189
I
II
p
p

194
I
II
mf

199
I
II
dim.

204
I
p

H
208
I
II
mf
p

212
I
II
p
p

215
I
cresc.
mf
I
II

219
I
II

223
I
II

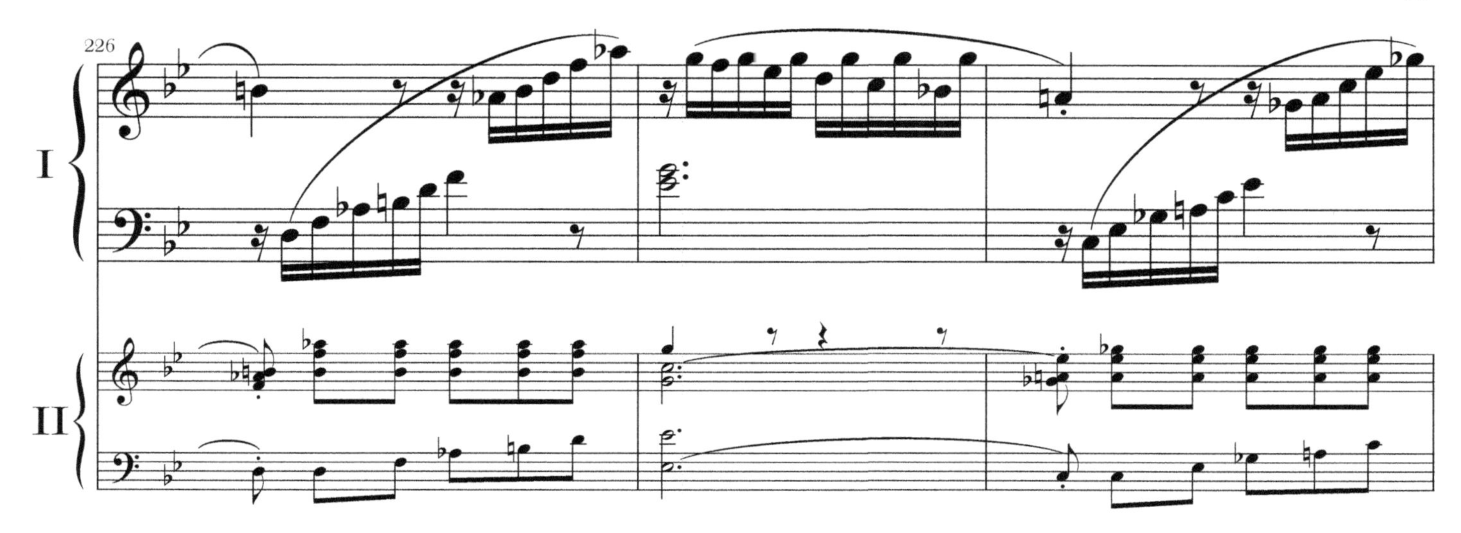
226
I
II

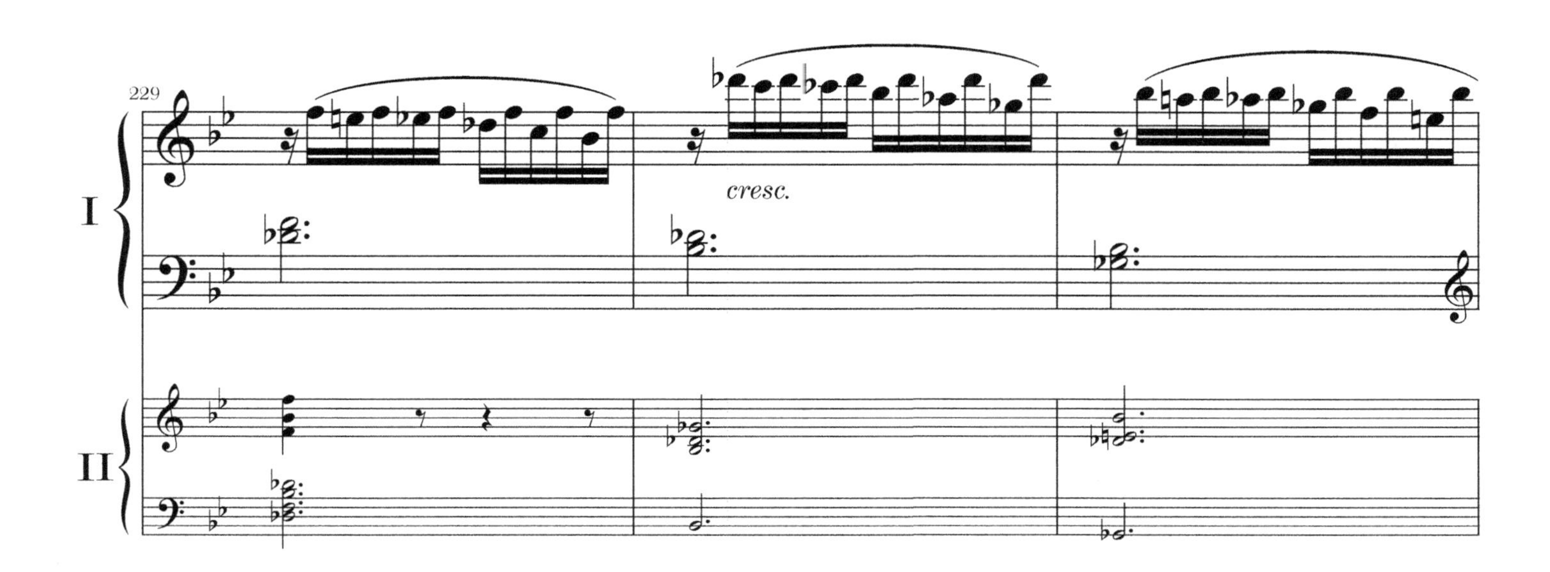
229
I
cresc.
II

232
I
f
II

236
K
I
Tutti
II

241
I
una corda
II

244
I
tre corde
II

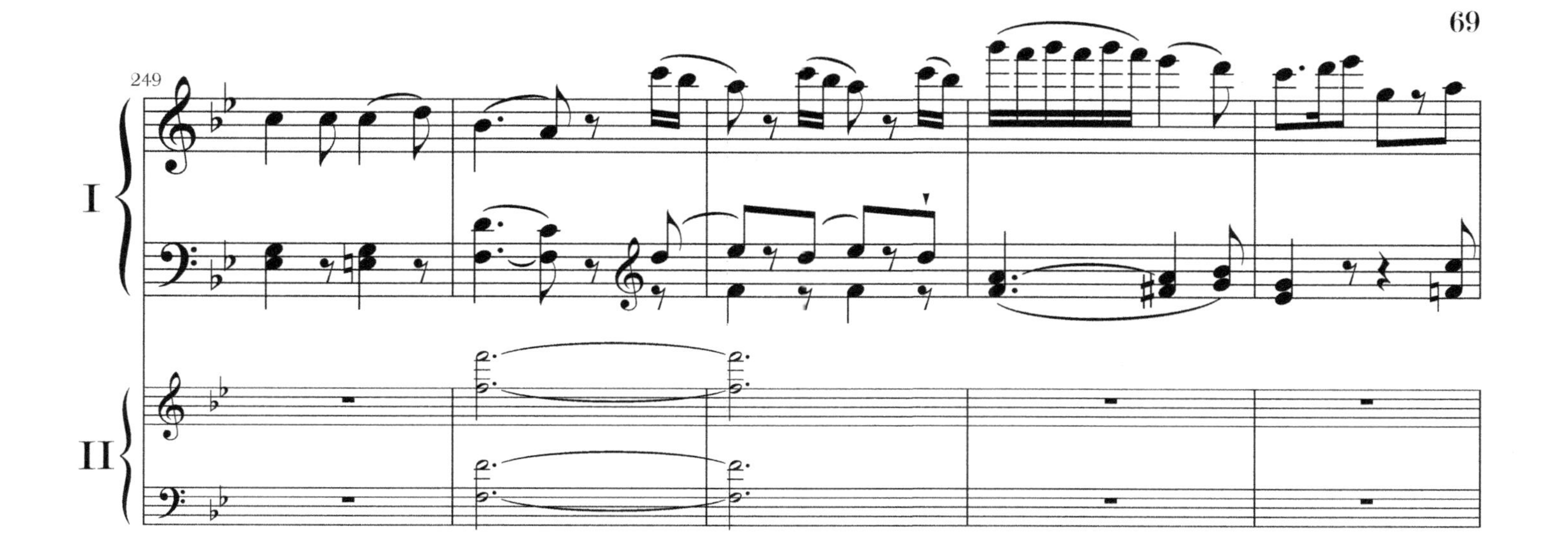
249
I
II

254
mf
I
II

258
I
II

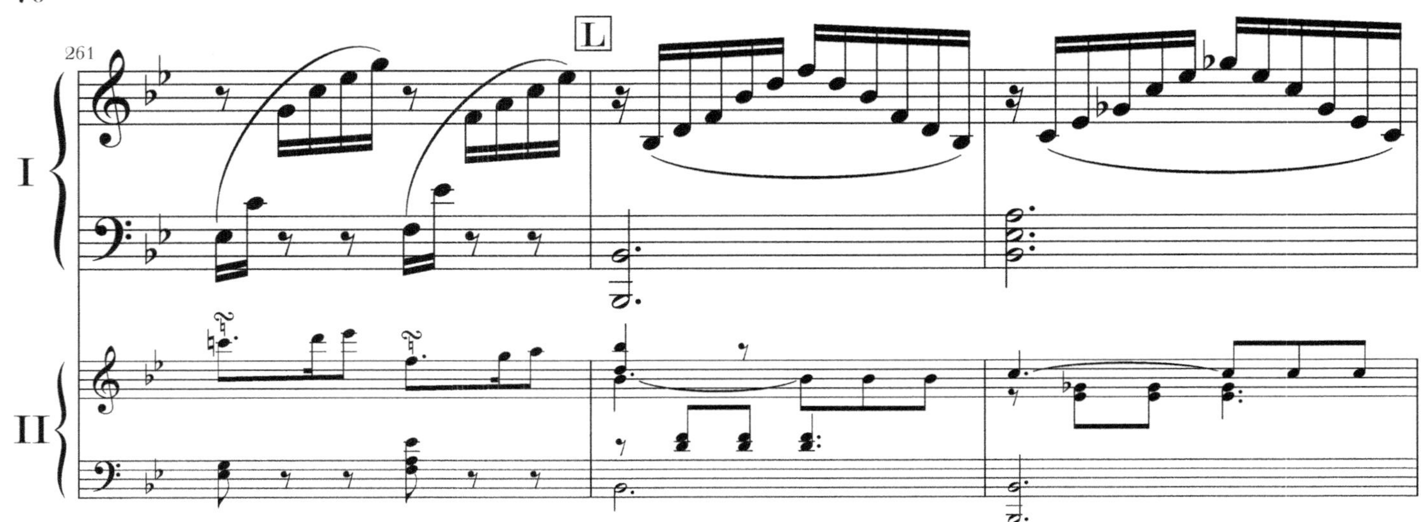
261
L
I
II

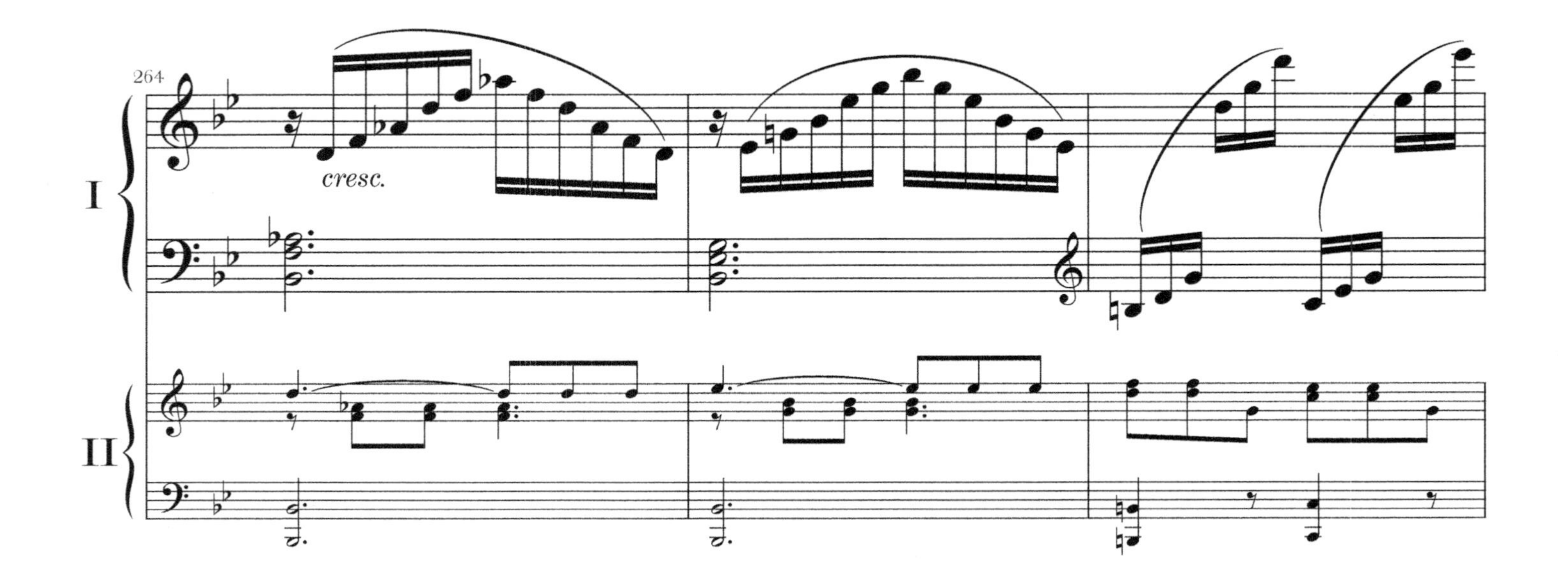
264
cresc.
I
II

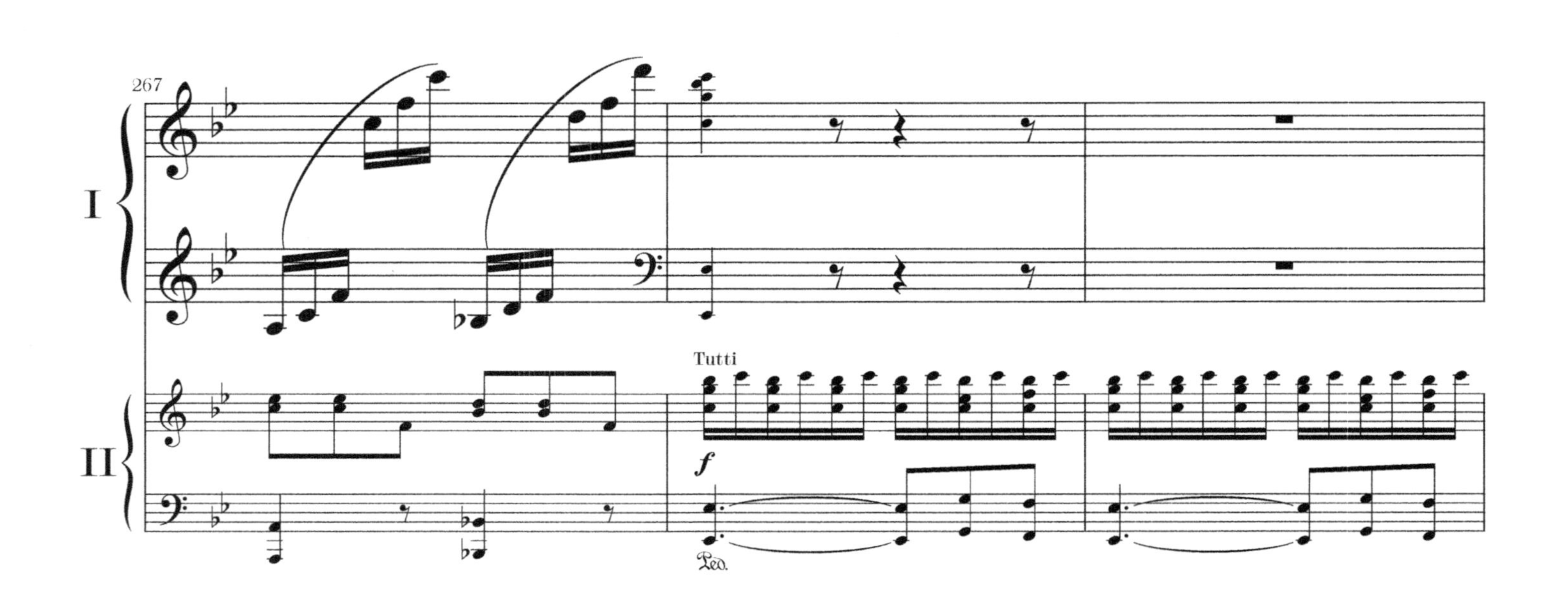
267
I
Tutti
II
f

Cadenza by W.A.Mozart

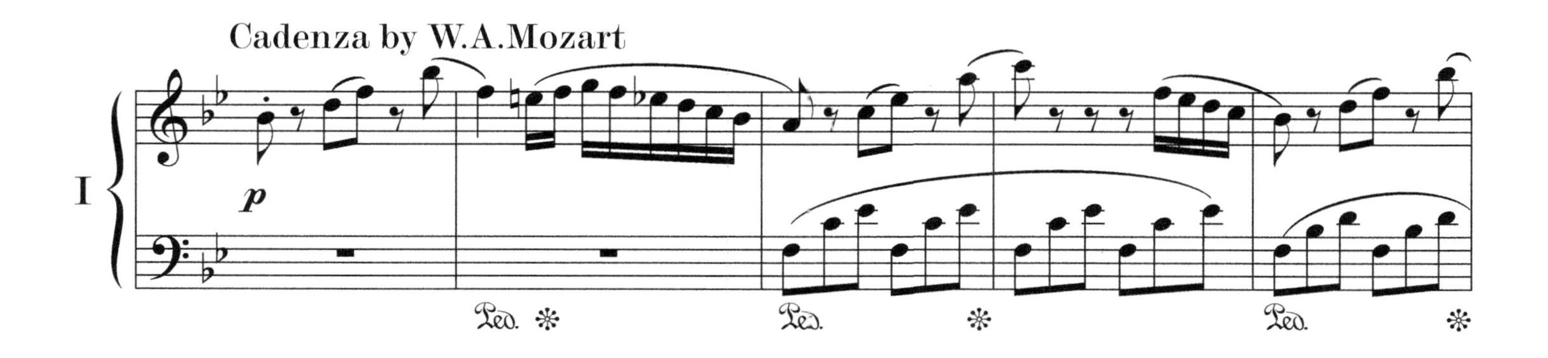

I
sf
f
sempre cresc.
Ped.
Ped.
Ped.
Ped.

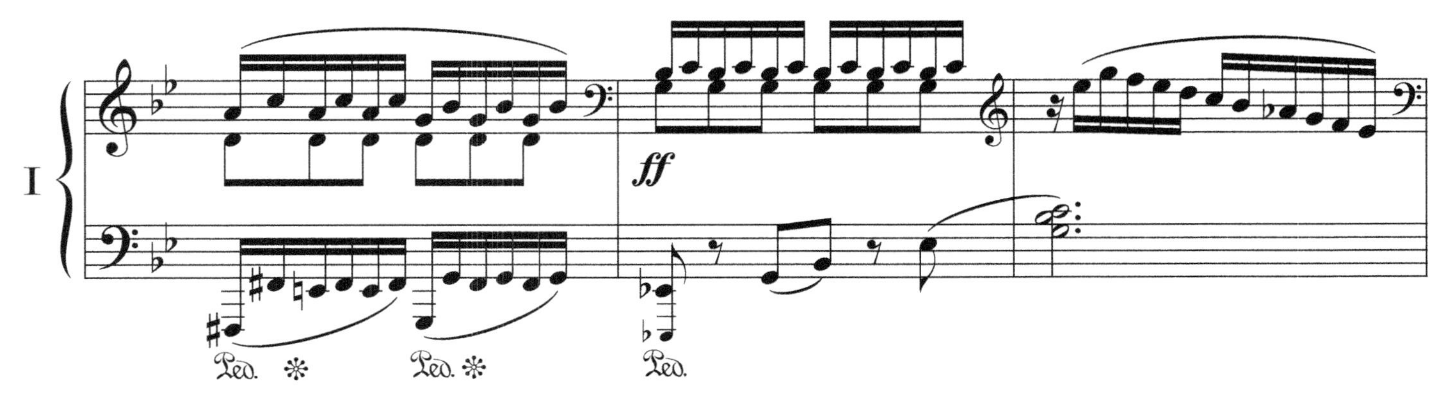
I
ff
Ped.
Ped.
Ped.

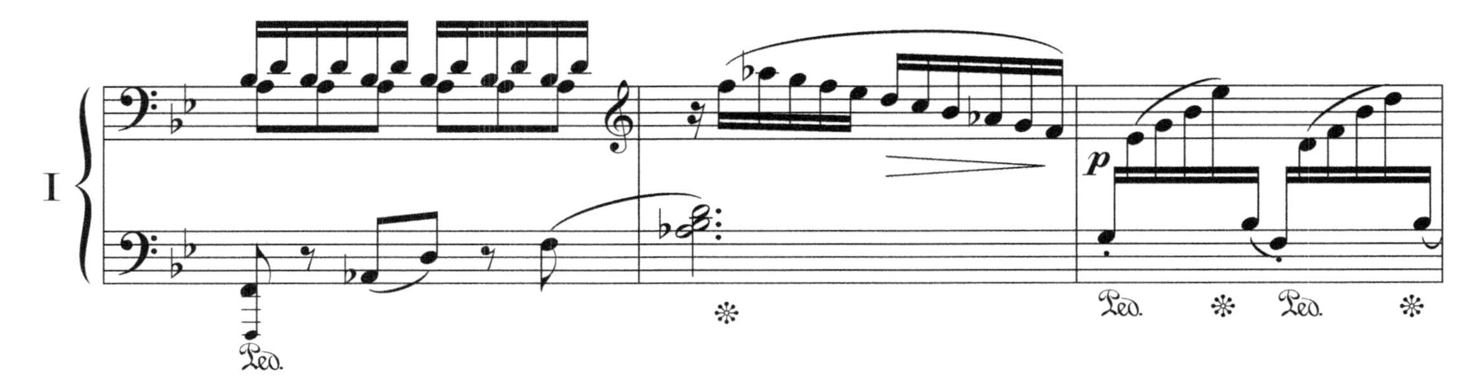
I
p
Ped.
Ped.
Ped.

I
cresc.
molto cresc. e ritard.
Ped.
Ped.
Ped.
Ped.
Ped.
Ped.

ritardando e poco a poco in tempo
I
sf
sempre ff

rit.
I
p
Ped.

rit.
poco a poco accelerando
I
dim.
p
Ped.
Ped.

I
cresc.
sf
Ped.
Ped.
Ped.
Ped.

tr
I
Ped.
senza Pedale

I
p
molto cresc.
Ped.

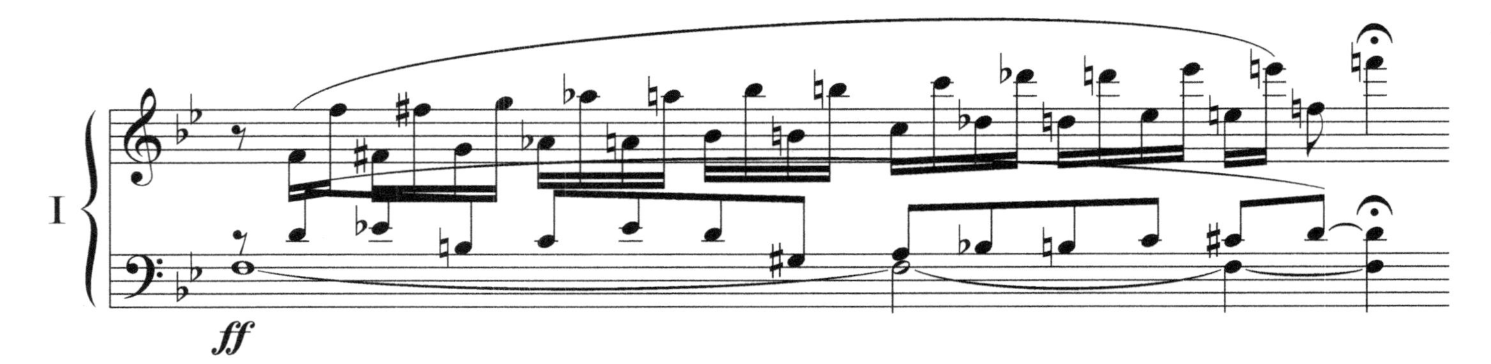
I
ff

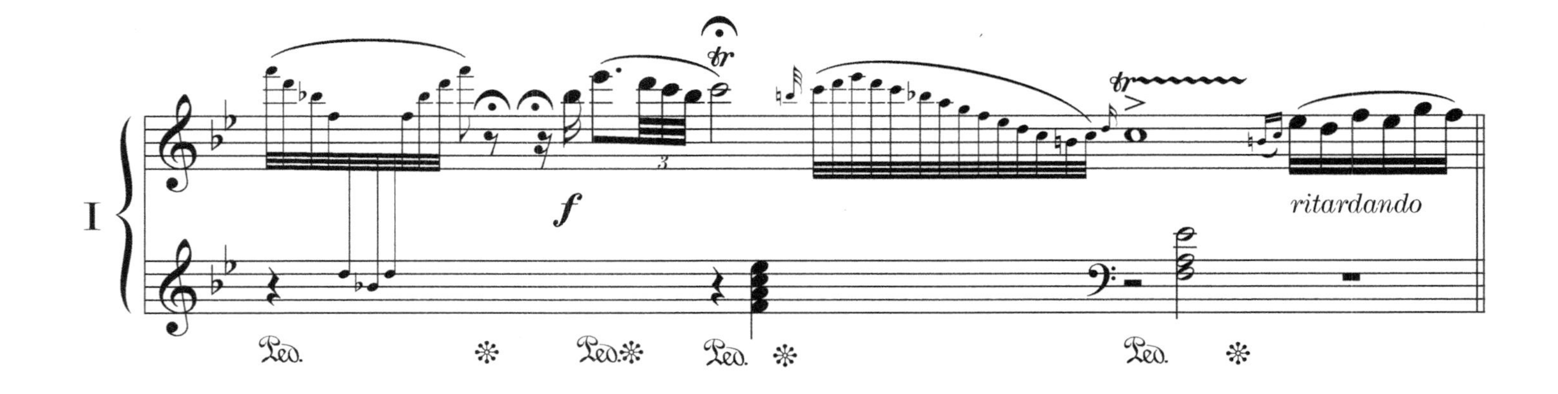
I
f
ritardando

273
I
p
legato

278
I
mf
Solo
II
p

283
I
II

288
I
II

292
I
II

297
I
II

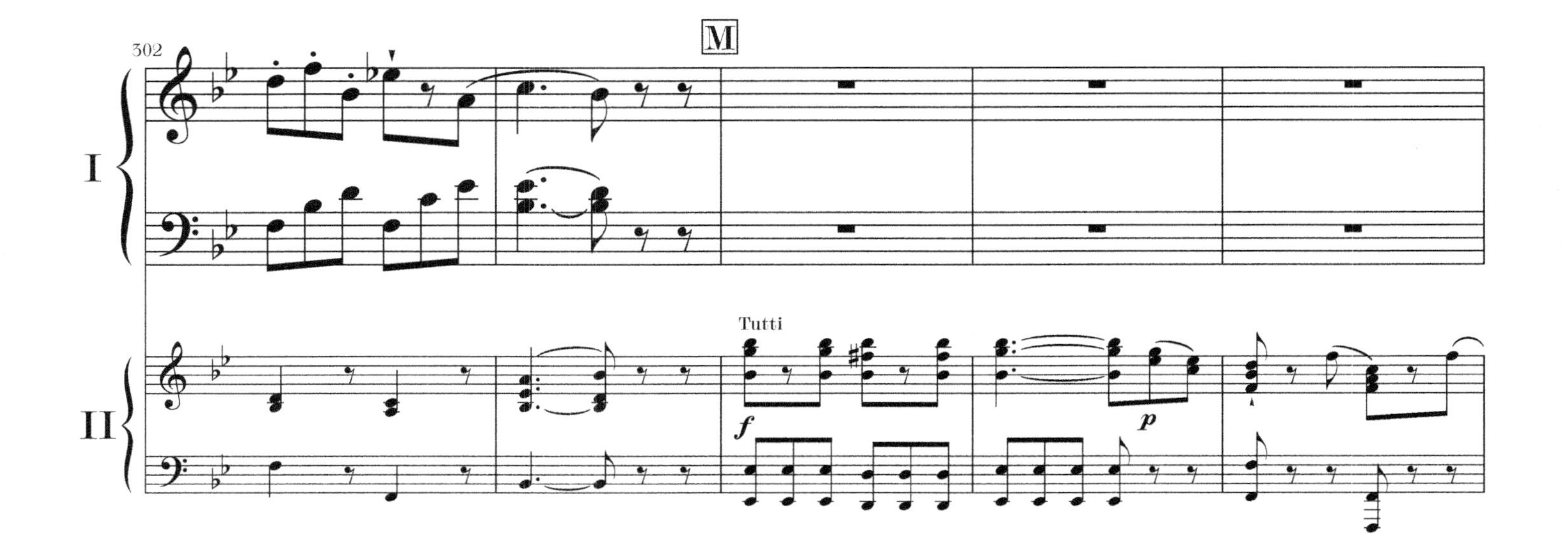
302
M
I
Tutti
f
p
II

307
II
f

312
II
p
f

316

II

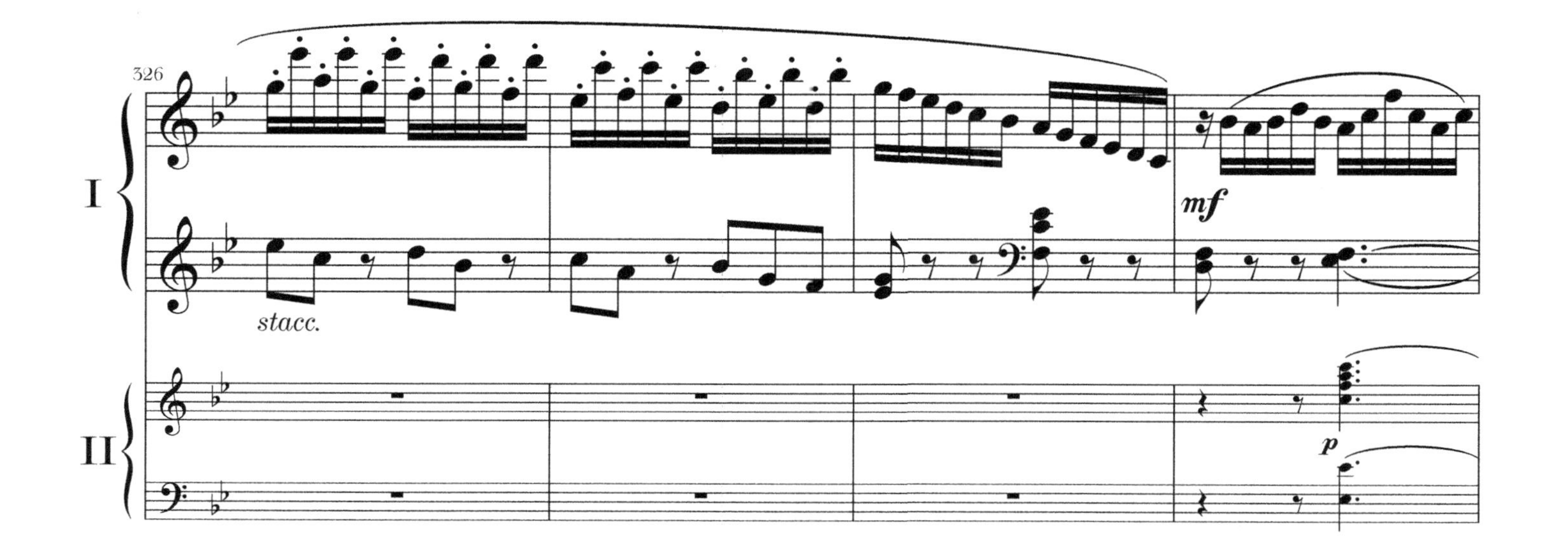

330
I
II
cresc.

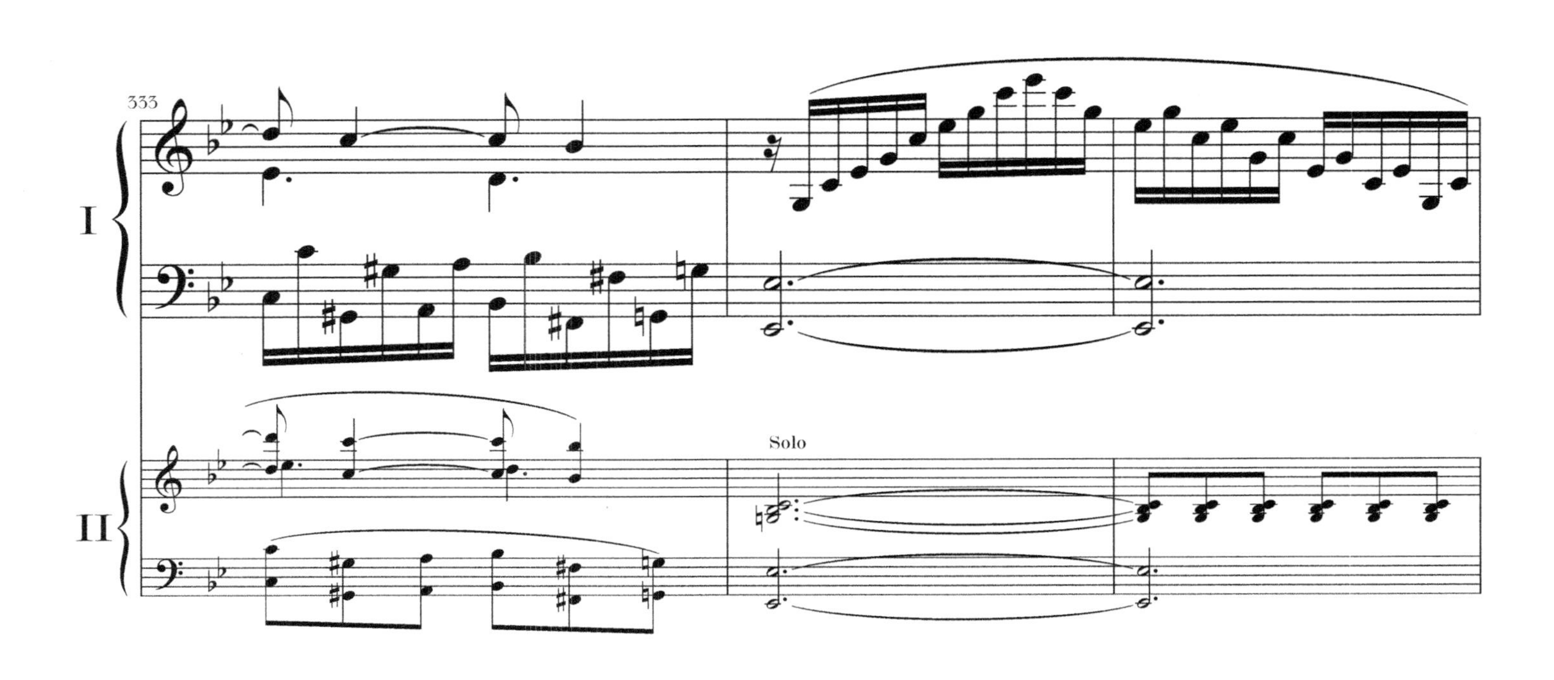
333
I
II
Solo

336
I
II
N
ff
f

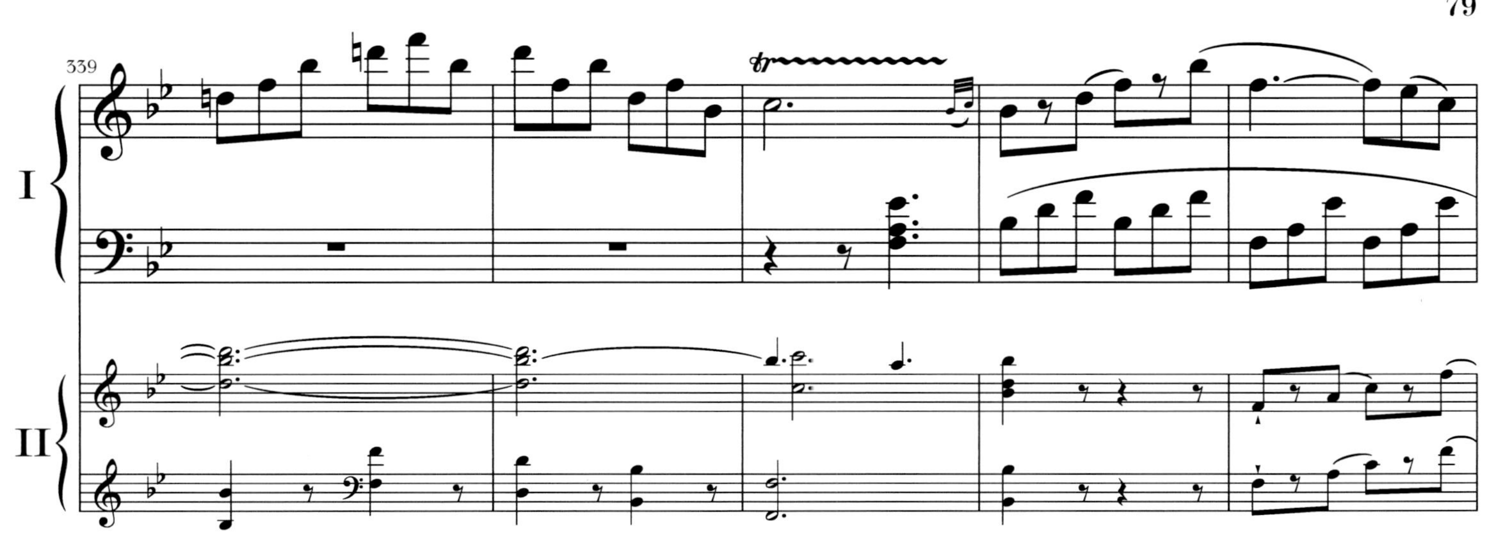
339
I
II

344
I
II

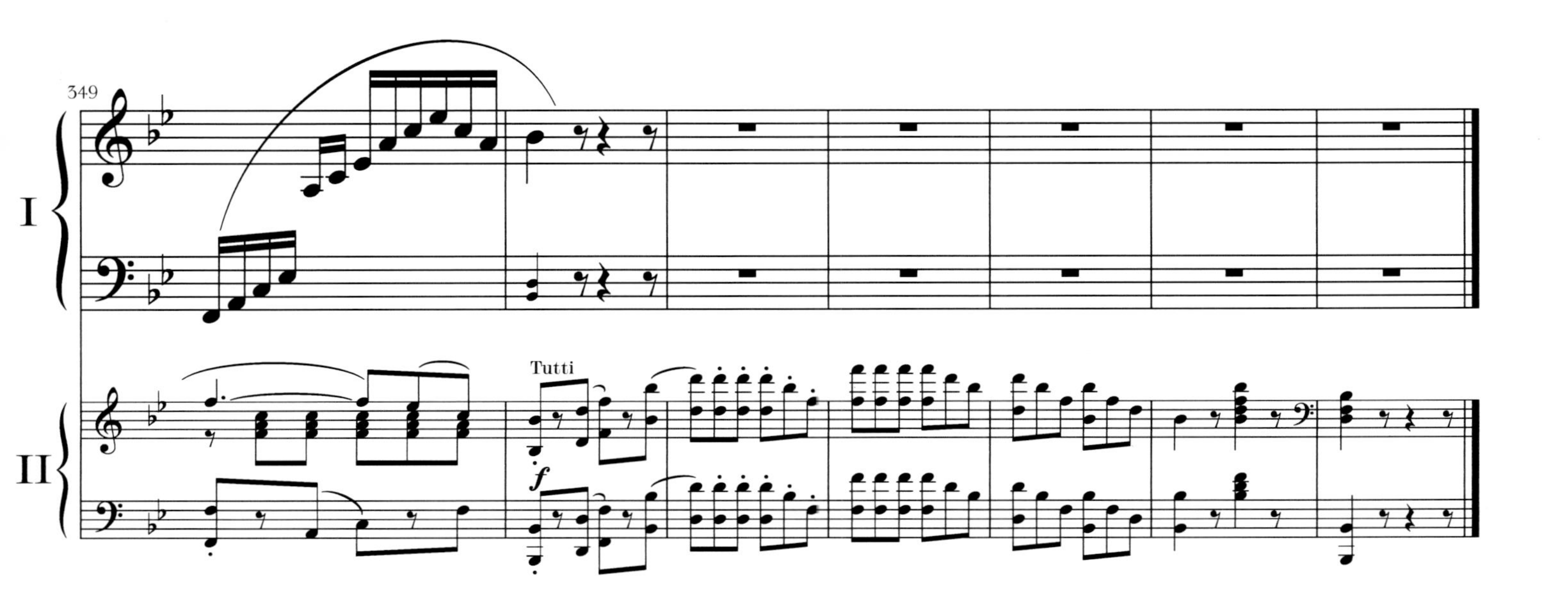
349
I
II
Tutti

MORE GREAT CLASSICAL PIANO PUBLICATIONS FROM

JOHANN SEBASTIAN BACH

Concerto in D Minor, BMV1052
Performed by David Syme, piano
Accompaniment: Stuttgart Festival Orchestra
Conductor: Emil Kahn
00400010 Book/Online Audio $22.99

Concerto in F Minor, BMV1056 & Concerto in E-Flat Major (J.C.F. Bach)
Performed by David Syme, piano
Accompaniment: Stuttgart SymphonyOrchestra
Conductor: Emil Kahn
00400009 Book/Online Audio $22.99

LUDWIG VAN BEETHOVEN

Concerto No. 1 in C Major, Op. 15
Performed by David Syme, piano
Accompaniment: Stuttgart Symphony Orchestra
Conductor: Emil Kahn
00400001 Book/Online Audio $24.99

Concerto No. 2 in B-Flat Major, Op. 19
Performed by David Syme, piano
Accompaniment: Stuttgart Symphony Orchestra
Conductor: Emil Kahn
00400002 Book/CD Pack $14.95

Concerto No. 3 in C Minor, Op. 37
Performed by Milena Mollova, piano
Accompaniment: Plovdiv Philharmonic Orchestra
Conductor: Nayden Todorov
00400017 Book/Online Audio $19.99

Concerto No. 4 in G Major, Op. 58
Performed by Kevin Class, piano
Accompaniment: Stuttgart Symphony Orchestra
Conductor: Emil Kahn
00400003 Book/Online Audio $24.99

Concerto No. 5 in E-Flat Major, Op. 73
Performed by Milena Mollova, piano
Accompaniment: Plovdiv Philharmonic Orchestra
Conductor: Nayden Todorov
00400018 Book/Online Audio $27.99

Prices, contents, and availability subject to change without notice.

FREDERIC CHOPIN

Concerto in E Minor, Op. 11
Performed by David Syme, piano
Accompaniment: Stuttgart Symphony Orchestra
Conductor: Emil Kahn
00400006 Book/Online Audio $29.99

Concerto in F Minor, Op. 21
Performed by Raluca Stirbat, piano
Accompaniment: Plovdiv Philharmonic Orchestra
Conductor: Nayden Todorov
00400013 Book/Online Audio $22.99

EDWARD GRIEG

Piano Concerto in A Minor, Op. 16
Performed by Milena Mollova, piano
Accompaniment: Plovdiv Symphony Orchestra
Conductor: Nayden Todorov
00400115 Book/Online Audio $27.99

FELIX MENDELSSOHN

Concerto No. 1 in G Minor, Op. 25
Performed by David Syme, piano
Accompaniment: Stuttgart Symphony Orchestra
Conductor: Emil Kahn
00400199 Book/Online Audio $19.99

WOLFGANG AMADEUS MOZART

Concerto No. 20 in D Minor, KV466
Performed by Kevin Class, piano
Accompaniment: Stuttgart Symphony Orchestra
Conductor: Emil Kahn
00400202 Book/Online Audio $24.99

Concerto No. 21 in C Major, KV467 "Elvira Madigan"
Performed by Sabri Tulug Tirpan, piano
Accompaniment: Vidin Philharmonic Orchestra
Conductor: Nayden Todorov
00400239 Book/Online Audio $19.99

Concerto No. 23 in A Major, KV488
Performed by Martin Stambalov, piano
Accompaniment: Plovdiv Philharmonic Orchestra
Conductor: Nayden Todorov
00400016 Book/Online Audio $27.99

SERGEI RACHMANINOV

Concerto No. 2 in C Minor, Op. 18
Performed by Frederick Moyer, piano
Accompaniment: East West Quantum Leap Orches
00400004 Book/Online Audio $24

Concerto No. 3 in D Minor, Op. 30
Performed by Alexander Raytchev, piano
Accompaniment: Plovdiv Philharmonic Orchestra
Conductor: Nayden Todorov
00400241 Book/Online Audio $24

Rhapsody on a Theme of Paganini
Performed by Alexander Raytchev, piano
Accompaniment: Plovdiv Philharmonic Orchestra
Conductor: Nayden Todorov
00400604 Book/Online Audio $27

FRANZ SCHUBERT

Quintet in A Major, Op. 114 D667 "The Tro
Performed by Harriet Wingreen, piano
Accompaniment: The Classic String Quartet
00400249 Book/Online Audio $22

ROBERT SCHUMANN

Concerto in A Minor, Op. 54
Performed by Kevin Class, piano
Accompaniment: Stuttgart Symphony Orchestra
Conductor: Emil Kahn
00400005 Book/Online Audio $22

PYOTR ILYICH TCHAIKOVSKY

Concerto No. 1 in B-flat Minor, Op. 23
Performed by David Syme, piano
Accompaniment: Stuttgart Symphony Orchestra
Conductor: Emil Kahn
00400011 Book/Online Audio $27

To see a full listing of Music Minus One publications and place your order from your favorite music retailer, visit
www.halleonard.com